BONSAI

The Art of Dwarfing Trees

BONSAI

The Art of Dwarfing Trees

By ANN KIMBALL PIPE

HAWTHORN/DUTTON
NEW YORK

BONSAI: THE ART OF DWARFING TREES

Library of Congress Catalog Card Number: 64-12439
ISBN: 0-8015-0796-0

10 11 12 13 14 15 16 17 18 19 20

To my friend
Nonkey T. Ishiyama,
of McLean, Virginia,
who has generously and patiently
taught me, over a period of years,
much that has gone into this book.

PREFACE

CREATING bonsai falls naturally into two parts, and this book has been divided accordingly. Learning to grow trees in pots, keeping them alive and healthy, is obviously the first step, but by no means the more important one. The second, shaping the trees into flowing lines and into arresting forms is the real art of bonsai, and cannot be learned from books alone any more than words alone can give a sculptor or painter the necessary feeling for line and color he will eventually gain from long practice and from studying the works of others.

This second step, however, is the one that is drawing more and more people to the growing of bansai, filling their needs to create lasting beauty in a medium as gratifying to the artist as any other in existence.

Though growing trees in pots satisfies the instinct in all of us to plant and water, to watch and enjoy, dwarfing and shaping trees is closer to sculpture than to any other art. An important difference between the two forms of expression is to be found in the constant changes that occur in bonsai; for while we rest, nature continues her work, reshaping and enlarging our trees, sometimes improving, sometimes not. She is an invaluable ally, but she must be watched. This very task, however, of watching and checking her enthusiasm increases our own and makes it impossible for the work ever to become too familiar or monotonous.

Because of this need for periodic reshaping, we often hear the words *infinite care* and *patience* in connection with the growing of

bonsai. In my opinion, these words have been overworked. In horti-
culture, lack of patience probably means lack of interest, for we do
not have to sit with folded hands waiting for a tree to grow. We
occupy ourselves with the business of living for most of our waking
hours. The tree, given reasonable care, grows along quietly whether
or not we are there to watch. Infinite care is unnecessary, too. Bonsai
require water, fresh air, occasional repotting, and protection from
the extremes of weather. What potted plants do not? The hours
spent in shaping and trimming them to reveal their beauty may be
as many or as few as we wish to give; trees do not die because we
cannot spare time today to shorten their tips or to wire their
branches. We can spare the time tomorrow, or next week. Sooner
or later if there is sufficient interest, the necessary hours will appear
as if by magic.

The first books to be published on bonsai, written in Japanese
and translated into English, gave only the "hows" of dwarfing trees
and none of the "whys." Because the subject had long been
shrouded in mystery, for beginners trying to follow such instructions it was "theirs not to reason why, theirs but to do and die."
When they read, for example, that the best soil for growing bonsai
was a hard substratum found only in Japan, which should be pul-
verized, sifted, and then sorted to select only such soil "as is granular
in form and of the uniform size of about one millimeter," it was
little wonder so many of them elected not "to do" at all.

As some growers in this country gained experience, they altered
the original rules and publicly spoke or wrote of their findings.
After a number of years there resulted a maze of contradictory rules
and regulations. Still lacking a clear explanation of principles, the
grower trying to evaluate these rules found that picking out uniform
granules of soil of about one millimeter in size seemed fairly simple
by comparison.

If you have been confused by such contradictory instructions, it
would be wise to remember that you were not necessarily reading
facts, but facts as each grower, based on his own experiences, saw

them. It does not follow that one was right and the others wrong, for there is more than one way to grow bonsai successfully. It does follow, however, that if you had no previous knowledge of the subject, you were left up in the air as to which methods to use. Obviously the best methods to use are the ones that will work for you.

In addition specific rules cannot be followed to the letter, because trees vary widely in the amount of abuse their roots will take and in their growth habits. Growing conditions vary not only from state to state, but from local area to local area, and often even from spot to spot in the same back yard.

For these reasons, I have long felt that the principles underlying the dwarfing of trees are as important, if not more so, than the actual process itself. Provided with these, common sense, and a simple, step-by-step description, any beginner with some gardening experience should be able to work out the variations best suited to his own climatic conditions and experience.

If the "rules" in this or any other book make sense to you, follow them. Flying out in all directions is a waste of time. But if you don't see why a thing must be done one way, do it another. If it works better your way, you have taken a long step forward. If not, you have learned a valuable lesson, for you never lose when you exchange one dead plant for a piece of knowledge that will later save eight, or perhaps ten plants.

In other words, do not have too much respect for authority. Learn what you can from it, then turn to the master teacher, Experience. His is the only word that cannot be disputed. To write before each sentence in this book, "I believe from my own experience that this is so," would make for very dull reading, but I hope you will mentally add these words to the printed ones as you go along.

I wish there were some way to write an informative book on any subject without allowing the intricate network of words to overpower the reader, leading him to believe the work ahead of him is more difficult than it really is. There doesn't seem to be such a way.

Keep in mind, however, that even a book on so simple a subject as growing zinnias would include detailed information on species, recommended soils, propagation methods, needs for light and water, and so on. The author would want to give all possible help so that the reader could grow as small or as elaborate a zinnia bed as he wished.

So it is with this book on bonsai. The information is here. Success does not depend on whether you use all of it.

CONTENTS

PART I

The Fundamentals of Growing Potted Trees

Chapter I

A POTTED TREE OR A BONSAI?

T HERE have been many explanations of the difference between a potted tree and a bonsai, and not all of them agree. Both
may be works of art; both may give the viewer a giant's eye glimpse
of a fairyland tree, faithful in every detail to its larger counterpart
in the forest; and both have undoubtedly been brought to perfection
by the skill of experienced growers.

As referred to in this book, a bonsai is a dwarfed, potted tree with
the smallest possible amount of soil supporting and nourishing the
largest possible trunk and branches. If the tree is planted in a container so roomy that the roots have plenty of space in which to grow
freely, it is called a potted tree.

A true bonsai must pass one other test. There is a Japanese word,
gei, for which no English substitute seems to exist. (Since Japanese
words are difficult for most Westerners to remember, it is the only
one used freely throughout this book.) *Gei* is the blending of com-
ponent parts into a pleasing and harmonious whole, the indefinable
quality that distinguishes true art from the mediocre. As such it is
recognized more readily by the trained eye. Freely, it is style, personality, charm; the quality of which J. M. Barrie wrote, " . . . if you have
it you don't need to have anything else; and if you don't have it, it
doesn't much matter what else you have."

Two small trees, side by side, may be very similar in shape and size; yet one may have *gei*, the other not, and even an expert can be hard pressed to explain the difference. But it will be there and he will feel it.

Just as one's taste improves as one listens to more and more of the world's fine music or studies its great paintings, so will his ability to recognize *gei* improve if he continues to study as many pictures as possible of the beautiful, ancient bonsai now in existence.

If he follows the normal pattern, the beginner will feel that the first trees he pots and trains are all that could be desired; and so they will be to him. If he has done his best, the pleasure he gets from the creative work will not be lessened one iota by the fact that his best will soon be at a higher level.

Training the eye to see is not difficult; interest and practice are the only requirements. On his first visit to the nursery, the forest, or the field in search of promising material, the novice may well be confused by the similarity of the plants before him. But without this first visit there can be no second, or tenth, or twentieth, when choice from such a wealth of material will no longer be confusing and he can quickly select a few promising specimens or the one best tree of them all.

There will certainly come a day when he will know almost at a glance if a particular tree, covered as it may be with bushy growth or distracting branches, will have *gei* after it has been properly trained and cared for. On that day he will no longer be a novice.

Bonsai are not necessarily very small trees. They are usually classified into four groups, large, medium, small, and miniature (or *mame*) bonsai and may range in height from more than three feet to just a few inches. This classification, however, is arbitrary and dictated by custom. There could just as well be three or five groups, for there is no sharp dividing line between them. The size of the tree does not matter, but the proportions do; the ratio of height to trunk size is of far more importance than either factor alone.

In addition to size, bonsai are traditionally classified by style—upright, slanting, semicascade, or fully cascade—and by whether a planting is formal or informal. Again, these categories are arbitrary. There are no clear lines of demarcation, and unless one is interested in following tradition for its own sake, such groupings are of little importance to American growers of bonsai. If too much is made of classification by size or style, the beginner may have a tendency to force his own ideas on the shape of the tree, whereas the natural characteristics of the tree itself should dictate what its final shape will be. If the finished tree is a successful bonsai, he may then call it anything he wishes.

Nor does the age of the tree deserve the importance attached to it by so many, particularly by those who have recently become interested in the subject. It is not difficult to differentiate between the quality of a bonsai ten or fifteen years old and a mature tree of fifty years or more; but when the difference narrows down to a few years, not even the expert can tell which is the older tree. The interest in age then becomes purely psychological. There is something impressive, even romantic, in the realization that such a small tree has been growing in such a small pot for so many years, and the more years the better.

A visit to a professional grower and seller of bonsai will soon educate the uninitiated concerning age. An eighty-year-old juniper was recently sold by a dealer in California for two hundred dollars. Next to it an elm, fifteen years younger, was priced at fifteen hundred dollars. The difference was in the perfection of the trees, in their *gei*, and in the years of attention to detail that had gone into the training of each. The elm was well worth more than seven times the price of the juniper. It is skill, then, and not age that counts the most. A five-year-old bonsai can be more attractive than one two or three times that age.

One other point about which there is widespread misunderstanding concerns the species of trees grown as bonsai. Many people who have heard of dwarfed trees and "Ming" trees connect the two and believe the Ming is a species of Japanese tree of which all bonsai are grown. On the contrary, the widely sold Ming tree is not a living tree at all, but an arrangement of twisted dead wood, artificial leaves, flowers, and moss, combined to resemble living, dwarfed trees. Bonsai are not limited to any one species; maples, elms, pines, cedars, junipers, and spruces, to name a few, have all been used with equal success.

Much has been written in recent years about "American bonsai" as opposed to Japanese. The best bonsai of Japan are so nearly perfect, however, that any attempt the American grower makes to be different can only be on the path away from perfection. Piling stones helter-skelter at the base of a tree, regardless of species, and adding buildings, fences, and figures may be unusual, but to say it is not always an improvement is an understatement.

On the other hand, many methods the Japanese have been using for hundreds of years are unnecessarily tedious and time-consuming. Here the American grower can exercise his natural talent for finding short cuts and more efficient ways to reach a common goal, that of creating lasting, living beauty in miniature.

Since, therefore, he cannot grow better or different bonsai than the Japanese have already grown, it seems sensible for the American to try to produce bonsai that are just as good and to do it in as few years as possible.

To that end he must first find a tree to work with.

An Alpine fir, still young and in its training pot, already has the twisted curves of an old, wind-swept tree.

Chapter II

START WITH A TREE

THERE is no species of tree that will not become somewhat dwarfed if its roots are confined in a pot and its top growth is trimmed back repeatedly. The results of such treatment, however, are not always pleasing, for fruits, leaves, and flowers do not become dwarfed as readily as do trunks and branches. If the purpose, therefore, is to achieve the effect of a truly miniature tree with all its parts in perfect proportion, it is best to start with one whose leaves, fruits, and flowers are naturally small.

It is not difficult to find such a tree. For example, of the many species of pines available to the grower, a large number have needles that do not normally grow longer than one or two inches, and will be still shorter when dwarfed. Siberian and Chinese elms have small leaves, though the American elm does not. Leaves of the white oak may be nine inches long, those of the cork oak two or three inches. The Norway maple has very large leaves, the trident maple very small ones. The Atlas cedar has shorter needles and denser growth than the Deodar cedar and is therefore more desirable as bonsai material. Among the conifers most cypresses, firs, spruces, cryptomerias, larches, and junipers have short needles. There are large- and small-flowering azaleas and fruit trees, large- and small-leaved rhododendrons and hollies. Small-berried plants such as pyracanthas and cotoneasters may be found in abundance. In addition, dwarf varieties of many large-leaved and large-fruiting species are now found in almost any nursery.

This is not to say that a tree with rather large leaves must be ruled out entirely for training as a bonsai. It would be a mistake to pass by an aged, naturally dwarfed tree with a beautiful trunk simply because its leaves were too large, or to ignore a nursery-grown tree with an unusual shape or some other attractive feature because of the size of its leaves.

Then, too, some growers of bonsai do not limit themselves to developing plants for the sole purpose of creating the illusion of perfect trees in miniature. They take equal pleasure in watching a tree develop its own natural characteristics and do not consider a pine unattractive because its needles are out of proportion to its trunk size or a pomegranate or plum tree less appealing if its fruit is somewhat large and heavy for its branches. The fondness many growers show for the Japanese black pine is an example; this species does not make a perfectly proportioned miniature tree, but when properly trained is as much admired as any other.

In short, suitable species for bonsai are plentiful; the shape of the tree one selects is of far more importance.

There are six major sources of trees suitable for bonsai, and choosing among them is a matter of personal preference. From the standpoint of the beginner whose horticultural experience has been limited to house plants or a home garden, the following list is arranged in order, starting with the simplest and most timesaving source of them all:

Nursery-grown trees in containers
Trees found growing naturally
Trees from rooted cuttings
Trees started from seed
Grafted trees
Trees from layering

A short discussion of the advantages and disadvantages of each source should give the reader an idea which most nearly suits his taste, experience, and available time.

The thick, bulging trunk makes this red-leaved barberry appear quite old, yet it was found in a nursery just two years before this picture was made.

Nursery-grown trees

There are three major advantages to starting with a tree grown in a nursery.

First, it has been transplanted at least once, often more, and its roots have not had a chance to become as long and spreading as those of trees found growing naturally. The shock of its first root-trimming and planting in a pot is thus lessened and its chance for survival greatly increased.

The wide selection of nursery trees is the second advantage and an important one. If the grower is particularly interested in finding a small spruce, for example, he can count himself lucky if he comes upon two or three promising ones in the woods. In a reasonably large nursery he may find not only from fifty to a hundred spruces, but also a wide range of species. Many nurseries offer the Colorado blue, Koster blue, Black Hills, Norway, white, and Alberta spruces, to name a few. He will also find, growing side by side, species that come from areas hundreds or thousands of miles apart. He may bring home, after a few hours of shopping, a shore pine, a live oak, an Atlas cedar, and a trident maple, trees native respectively to the Rocky Mountains, the southern United States, North Africa, and China or Japan. Even the grower who loves to travel in search of plant material has his limits, and he surely would have reached them before he could gather together such a varied collection.

The third advantage of starting with a nursery tree is that it can save time, often many years, for the home grower. There is a popular notion that it is useless to become interested in growing bonsai after one has reached an advanced age because not enough years are left in which to produce an ancient tree. This is poor reasoning. One could as accurately say there is no use in rearing children because one may not live to enjoy them in their old age. Every step of the way is a pleasure, and many young trees, if properly trained, have more *gei* and attract more admiration than others twice their age.

But age cannot be ignored completely, and it is not at all unusual to find a small nursery tree that is already ten or twelve years old. Needless to say, the saving of years, however many and for whatever purpose, is not to be taken lightly.

The one disadvantage in hunting for small trees in a nursery is that it is harder to find the unusual, twisted shapes so dear to the hearts of all bonsai growers. The average nursery tree is as straight and symmetrical as the grower was able to make it, for these qualities are the most popular for foundation and lawn plantings which constitute the great bulk of a nurseryman's business. In addition, the bark texture of nursery trees is comparatively smooth, and their trunks have few of the bumps and knots often found in natural specimens. However, there are many exceptions to this generality, and the search for them adds zest to the shopping trip.

A word should be added here about local versus mail-order nurseries. In every case but one it is better to shop locally. If a tree has been field-grown a few miles from home, the buyer can be sure it is adapted to his climate and will survive local winters and summers in his care as safely as it did in the nursery. Trees grown hundreds of miles from home may or may not be suited to his area. He has the advantage, also, of choosing from many shapes and sizes instead of having to accept whatever comes in the mail. More often than not, trees sent by mail have disappointing, pencil-sized trunks that require added years of training.

The one advantage to ordering from a catalogue is that large mail-order nurseries usually have a wider selection of hard-to-find species than can be found locally. If the buyer has been looking for a particular tree, ordering it by mail may be the only way he can obtain it.

He should beware, however, of exotic catalogue names that give no indication what the species really is. To advertise such names as "Morning Mist maple" or "Canton Contorted cherry" is completely unfair, for few bonsai addicts are able to resist these even though they may suspect they are being misled.

Now about thirteen years old, this dwarfed Mugho pine was developed from a nursery tree.

Weeping species of the European beech makes a graceful and easy-to-care-for bonsai.

A reputable mail-order nursery will give the botanical name of the tree or the commonly accepted name, such as "dawn redwood" or "Chinese elm." The "Morning Mist maple" may turn out to be a very common species that could have been bought in a better size and shape, and at less expense, just a few miles from home.

Trees found growing naturally

Many natural trees have survived the rigors of difficult growing conditions. Their roots have had to find sustenance in small crevices between rocks or bricks, in sun-baked fields, or on banks of streams where most of the soil has been washed away. No human hand has fed or watered them or cleared away the undergrowth with which they have had to compete to stay alive. As a result, many such trees are naturally dwarfed. Their trunks may be thick and twisted, their bark rough and weathered; they may be many years old and yet no more than one or two feet high. Unfortunately the bonsai enthusiast does not find such trees as often as he dreams of them. They do exist, however, and the mere possibility that a search for them may not be fruitless is reason enough for making it.

The advantages of such trees are obvious. In counting on them as the principal source of one's collection, however, there are two disadvantages: they are difficult to find, and often tricky to transplant. Methods of transplanting will be discussed later. It is sufficient to say here that one should be thoroughly familiar with such methods before attempting to move a mature, naturally dwarfed tree.

Of course many natural trees can be found growing under more favorable conditions. Such trees, from a few months to a few years old, can be found anywhere, in vacant lots, in woods and fields, in orchards, or in one's own garden hiding in shrubbery borders or behind foundation plantings. Though these will be comparatively young while still of a size suitable for training as bonsai, they can be very useful, particularly to the beginner. He can use them for experimental purposes and learn just how far he can go in trimming their roots without losing the trees. If he goes too far and does lose a few, it has been a very inexpensive lesson.

These young trees can also be increased in size by the short-cut method described in Chapter IX, and in a few years will be ready for potting and training as bonsai.

As its name suggests, the foliage of this Amur scarlet maple forest turns a fiery red in fall.

Trees from rooted cuttings

Plants grown from cuttings are necessarily small at the start and therefore take more time to grow into trees of a good size. However, like trees grown from seed, rooted cuttings are an excellent source for miniature bonsai. Unlike seedlings, they do not develop a tap root and are well adapted to planting in small, very shallow containers. Rooting a cutting is the best way by far to propagate certain species, particularly hybrids, where seedlings do not run true.

The pros and cons of propagating by cuttings are very likely to be an academic question, however, because no bonsai grower can force himself to discard entirely the rather formidable heap of branch ends he finds at his elbow after a pruning session. The fact that some months later he will find himself faced with more small plants than he knows what to do with is no deterrent whatever. His neighbors may welcome a few rooted cuttings from his prize ivy or begonia plant, but by the law of averages they are not likely to be bonsai enthusiasts, and it is difficult to find anyone else who will graciously accept a handful of rooted junipers or cypresses two or three inches tall. Nor can any true plant lover let them face death by neglect or strangulation. Advice: Do not root more cuttings than can be used.

Trees started from seed

As soon as the grower lets it be known he is interested in bonsai he will begin to receive seeds from friends. They will fall from Christmas-card envelopes, be tucked between pages of letters from all parts of the country, be brought to him from other countries by vacationing friends. Whether or not to plant tree seeds, therefore, becomes another academic question; there is no choice.

This can be both good and bad. Some seeds are bound to be unidentified. "It was growing just outside our hotel window and had the most lovely purple-pink flowers," are words to whet the curiosity of any bonsai lover, and some trees produced in this way turn out to be most unusual and well worth nursing along to maturity. Some seeds are of a species known to the recipient but unlisted in catalogues, and these, too, are often welcome. But some are from species that can be bought as good-sized trees for a dollar or two just a short distance from home. This presents a problem for which each recipient must find his own solution. The writer has none to offer.

To the grower interested in miniature bonsai, raising trees from seeds is a must. Along with cuttings it offers the only way to obtain plants that will fit into very small containers.

For purposes other than obtaining unusual species or tiny plants, however, growing trees from seeds is second best to other methods. Though it is entirely possible to produce a good-sized tree from seed in four or five years, this is often four or five years spent needlessly.

Grafted trees

Grafting, a method of combining the most desirable qualities of two trees by inducing a shoot of one to grow on the roots or trunk of another, has many advantages, one disadvantage. Some bonsai growers shun grafted trees because they claim the scar left at the point of union is unsightly and never disappears entirely. Many beautiful old bonsai were started from grafts, however, and since grafting may be done on the roots or at the top of the tree where it will not show, this argument seems unsound. In addition, as the tree ages, graft marks made on very young stock do tend to disappear to the point where they are not noticed.

In its favor, grafting can solve many problems facing the grower. Its principal use is to combine the beauty or superior fruiting or flowering qualities of one species with the sturdiness or fast-growing qualities of another. The attractive five-needle pine is an example. It grows very slowly from seed and when young is quite delicate. When grafted onto the trunk of the Japanese black pine, however, it increases in size more quickly and does not require ideal growing conditions in order to survive.

The procedure may be reversed, if desired. Grafting a fast-growing tree on dwarf stock will help to slow and stunt its growth. If the shape of a valued bonsai can be improved by the addition of a branch on the trunk, grafting will produce it. Fruit trees grown from seed usually take many more years to bear fruit than do those produced by grafting. Hybrid varieties can easily be propagated by grafting.

It is a good idea for the grower to understand the pros and cons of grafting even though he may not wish to learn the process. Many nursery trees are produced by grafting, and although the purchaser may not know why the grafting was done, he can be fairly certain the professional grower has somehow improved the species by doing it. His only concern, then, is whether or not the graft mark is conspicuous enough to make the tree undesirable as a future bonsai.

Trees from layering

Layering, a method by which a branch is induced to grow roots while still attached to the parent tree, is highly recommended by many botanist-authors. However, it is not widely practiced by many beginners in bonsai, because for them it has one major disadvantage: it seldom works.

The exceptions are easy-to-propagate species, most of them deciduous, which will also root easily from cuttings. From several months to several years may pass before the results of layering are known. If successful, the branch must then be cut from the parent tree and planted elsewhere without injuring the fresh, delicate roots.

If the grower has a favorite tree in his yard and cannot find a smaller one of the same species elsewhere, layering may be the only method by which he can obtain it. Otherwise he is starting his bonsai the hard way.

Selecting a nursery tree

It is very easy to find excellent bonsai material in almost any nursery. It is more difficult to recognize it. Though there is no substitute for practice in training the eyes to see, a check list and a short discussion of important points will serve as a guide for the beginner. In the order of importance, he should consider:

Trunk
Branches
Leaf size
Tree size
Container size
Species

TRUNK

The trunk should be examined first. It is the most important feature of practically any bonsai. The thicker it is, the better. Its length and shape must also be considered, for no matter how thick it is, if leaf growth starts two or three feet above soil level, or if it has an uninteresting shape, it will not make a good bonsai. If the tree is young and supple, its trunk can be shaped with wires and ties to suit the grower; but if it is stiff and hard, it will probably hold its shape for the life of the tree. The buyer should ask himself if it will be as pleasing to him in all the years to come as it was at first sight.

There are no rules as to whether a trunk must be straight or curved, twisted or smooth-flowing, horizontal or perpendicular. The only requirement is that it should have *gei*, and in general a trunk with an unusual line is more likely to have it, for naturally dwarfed trees are seldom straight and erect. There are exceptions, however, and one's own taste is his best guide.

Very often, especially in nursery stock, the base of a trunk may be concealed below soil level or covered with wood shavings or moss.

It is not unusual to find that after a new tree has been potted it has lost its *gei* because its trunk is several inches longer than it appeared to be when purchased. On the other hand, an examination of the concealed trunk base may show that the tree will be more attractive when potted than it is in its present container.

It is also easy to be misled by the thick growth of branches that may cover the tree. These should be pushed aside and only the trunk considered for this first examination. If it is a good one, the tree has passed its most important test.

BRANCHES

In general, the lowest branches of a tree should be the heaviest. Not only does this follow nature's usual pattern but as the tree ages its vitality tends to move from the lower to the upper branches. If a low branch is weak to begin with, it may eventually die.

Thin bottom branches do not look natural and may die as tree ages.

Heavy bottom branches look more natural, are more likely to survive.

The locations of branches on a conifer are more important than those on a deciduous tree. A deciduous tree can be encouraged to develop new branches by judicious pruning, but most conifers cannot.

Whether the tree under consideration has many branches or few, it is almost certain to need pruning before its shaping is completed. On-the-spot, detailed planning of pruning is an impossible task, for very often the necessity for one step does not appear until after a preceding one has been taken. However, the heaviest, main branches will probably not be removed, so they should be studied carefully. Their lines can be changed later with wires, ties, and pruning, but their relative thicknesses and positions on the trunk will always remain the same.

LEAF SIZE

The importance of leaf size has already been discussed. It is sufficient to say here that it is one of the points that should be considered when selecting a tree for bonsai.

TREE SIZE

If the tree selected has all the other requirements of promising bonsai material but is too tall, the trunk may be reduced to the desired height provided the evidence of such an operation will not show. A heavy, mature trunk should not be cut back to such an extent that its width at the top nearly equals its base width. Since a trunk normally tapers gradually from base to tip, one whose entire length is of uniform thickness can spoil the *gei* of the tree as much as if the cut itself were visible. This is less important with the thin trunk of a young tree. The trunk will gradually thicken at the base as it matures.

Before purchasing a too tall tree, the grower can easily determine in advance if its height can be reduced successfully. Does it branch low on the trunk? Is there a noticeable thinning of the trunk between its base and the point at which it will be cut off? Will there be enough remaining branches behind which the necessary cut can be concealed? Similarly, can the cuts on heavy branches that need to be shortened be made at points where smaller branches join them, so that they can be concealed?

A trunk with no variation in width indicates the top has been sawed off.

A tapering trunk, as shown, is one sign of a good bonsai.

As a rule, a tree that has been allowed to grow to a desired height is more apt to have *gei* than one that has been cut back. But there are many exceptions, and these are well worth looking for, since they can save years of work for the grower.

The ten-inch ginkgo shown below was more than three feet tall when purchased, and this picture was taken only six weeks later. In spite of its original height, the trunk starts to taper one inch or so above its base, and the lowest branch is just one-and-a-third inches from soil level. These two points made the tree a good purchase. There are many more like it waiting to be recognized in nurseries all over the country.

CONTAINER SIZE

The size of the container in which the tree is growing will, of course, determine the amount of work the purchaser faces before his tree is in its final pot. It is perfectly feasible to reduce a two-gallon- or even a five-gallon-size root ball to one that will fit into a small container, but this will take time. Only a certain number of roots can safely be cut off in one season, and the greater the discrepancy between a tree's first and final containers, the greater the number of steps necessary to make the change.

The most practicable, and therefore the most popular, container is the one-gallon size. It is easy to handle, the work of reducing the root ball is simplified, and most nurseries offer the largest selection in this size.

SPECIES

It is a simple matter to recommend a particular species or variety of tree for bonsai, usually a much more difficult one to find it. The Japanese five-needle pine, for example, is often referred to in books as "popular," yet the writer has been able to find young specimens of it in only two nurseries, on opposite sides of the country. Many other species are equally difficult to find. In fact, the average grower, thumbing through a few catalogues and shopping at local nurseries, may count himself lucky if he finds even a small percentage of his list of desirable species. In addition, anyone who writes about bonsai has a few trees of which he is especially fond. There is a natural tendency to recommend these species, though usually there are others with equally desirable qualities.

It seems more sensible, then, not to recommend species at all. A tree need only fit the requirements of good bonsai material and, for the beginner, be reasonably easy to grow. The list of trees in Chapter XIII will give the reader an idea of the special qualities of each genus. With this information he can then select trees that will most nearly suit his taste and experience.

Bringing home a natural tree

The check list for judging potential bonsai material grown in nurseries applies equally well to natural trees. But in addition to selecting a natural tree, one must know how to dig it and bring it home safely.

There are three vital points to keep in mind when moving a tree from its original growing place. It should be dug at the proper time of year, with as many short side roots and attached fibrous roots as possible, and with an undisturbed ball of soil at the base of the trunk.

It is not always possible to fulfill all three conditions, and for a young or easily transplanted tree, not always necessary. Many mature trees, however, resent having their roots disturbed, and if one finds an irreplaceable, natural dwarf, he will want to give it every possible chance to survive. The maximum safeguards will therefore be discussed, and the grower can then make whatever exceptions he thinks advisable when digging his own trees.

The best time to move a tree is during its dormant period, preferable near the end of it in early spring, just as the buds are beginning to swell.

Unfortunately many people try to transplant small trees in summer, when they are already in full leaf or flower. This is understandable, since trees are more attractive at that time and apt to catch the eye. Often, however, to move a mature, natural tree during its growing period is to condemn it to death. If a promising tree is found at this time, it should be marked for future digging and left untouched until the proper season.

Early fall is the second best time for transplanting. The tree will still have time to become established in its new location before winter comes, but generally the risk is greater in autumn than during the dormant period.

If a tree has been growing undisturbed for many years, its roots are apt to be long and spreading and many of the important fine, or fibrous, roots may be far from the base of the trunk. As a result, when the long side roots are cut back, there may not be enough fibrous roots left after transplanting to sustain the life of the tree.

The solution to the problem is fairly simple. By cutting through all but a few of the side roots in a circle ten to eighteen inches from the trunk, the distance depending on tree size, a new set of fibrous roots is encouraged to develop. Because roots tend to grow only in the region of the topsoil, which is seldom more than ten or twelve inches thick, a depth of about ten inches for the cut will be sufficient. The tree should then be left alone until the following spring, when the tap root and remaining side roots may be cut and the tree taken from the ground.

Side roots are severed in a circle twelve to eighteen inches from the trunk, about ten inches deep.

The following spring tap root and remaining side roots are cut and tree is lifted from the ground.

If the tree is quite old and valuable, or a hard-to-transplant conifer, spreading the root cutting over a period of two years is an extra
safety measure. A few side roots and the tap root may be cut one
season and the rest of the side roots the next. The tree is then taken
from the ground the following spring, at the end of the second year.
Since one function of the tap root is to anchor the tree in the
ground, when it is removed there is a danger that the tree will be
blown over by strong winds. Shortening and thinning the branches
will help it to maintain its balance until new, anchoring roots have
had time to grow.

The fibrous roots of a young tree do not present the same problem. As there are usually enough of them near the base of the trunk,
a young tree may be moved in one operation.

It is a fact, surprising to many, that in transplanting a tree it is
more important to keep an undisturbed ball of soil around shortened
roots than to retain them all intact but exposed.

This is not always easy to do. The roots of some plants, pyracanthas, cotoneasters, pines, and young maples among them, do not
hold soil readily when they are moved. In addition, some soils crumble easily, especially those in rocky or sandy areas. Any roots that
have been bared during digging should be covered with damp earth
immediately after the tree is lifted, and the whole ball wrapped in
burlap or heavy paper. The tree should then be replanted as soon as
possible.

The foregoing describes ideal conditions for transplanting, but
the ability of a tree to survive conditions far from ideal depends
largely on its age and species. A hardy, deciduous tree may safely be
dug bare-root, and the number of fibrous roots retained is of less importance than it is for a conifer. It may not, however, be safely dug in
the wrong season.

In digging a more difficult tree, a mature pine, for example, as
many maximum-safety conditions should be provided as possible. In
handling one-of-a-kind, valuable old trees one cannot err on the side
of caution.

A naturally dwarfed hackberry. Trees like this can be found often enough to make searching the fields and woods well worthwhile. Below, as it appeared before potting and trimming.

Though a natural tree may be potted as soon as it is brought home, it will have a better chance of survival if it is allowed to grow in the open ground for a year or more. It should be planted in a shaded corner of the garden and given the same treatment as that recommended for sick trees in Chapter VII. Here, as before, the importance of taking every precaution varies with the species and the value placed on the tree by the grower.

Rooting cuttings

Cuttings are usually classified by the condition of their wood. This, in turn, depends on the time of year they are taken from the parent plants. A softwood cutting, as the name implies, is still green and pliable and is cut from the plant in early spring. A half-ripewood cutting is taken in summer and a hardwood cutting in winter, when the plant is dormant. Authorities disagree so widely about which season is best for making cuttings that the combined recommendations of eight botanist-authors include all twelve months of the year. It is reasonable to assume, then, that cuttings can be made at almost any time.

Most of the writer's cuttings, from two to eight inches long, are made in early spring, at repotting time, principally because there is such an abundance of pruned ends, many of them already branched, from which to choose. These are put immediately into the cutting bed or into a pot filled with rooting medium. The rest are started in late fall, when hardened shoots are cut from the trees, buried in a box of sand, and stored in a cool room until spring. They are then treated the same as the newly cut shoots.

The rooting medium may be sharp river sand, or an equal mixture of sand and peat moss or sand and vermiculite. A hole a little larger and deeper than the lower half of the cutting is made in the wet sand with a stick. All leaf growth and buds are removed from the portion to be buried, but they are allowed to remain on the exposed upper section. The cut end and below-surface nodes are then moistened and dipped in a hormone rooting powder. The excess is tapped off so that only a light film remains. The shoot is then inserted in the sand to a depth of about half its length and the sand packed carefully around it with a stick. When all the cuttings have been inserted, each is watered to settle the sand evenly around the buried portions.

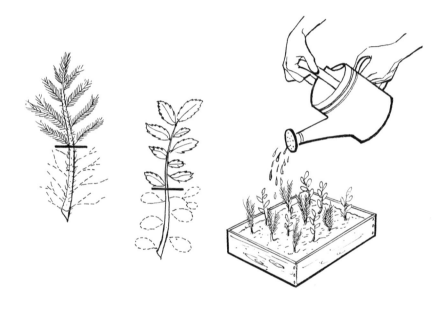

Foliage is removed below lines as shown.

Bared stems are inserted in rooting medium and watered.

An ideal cutting bed will furnish the following conditions: even, but not excess, moisture; light heat from below; high humidity for the exposed portions; protection from sun and wind; and a constant air temperature. Unless one has professional equipment, not all these conditions can be met, but the more that are, the higher the percentage of cuttings that will root.

There are so many differing lists of species that can and cannot be propagated from cuttings that the grower would be wise to ignore them all and try whatever trees he would like to have. With the exception of pines, which all agree cannot be rooted in this way, and of nut trees, which are difficult but not impossible to root, nearly all species can be rooted successfully from cuttings under the right conditions. If the attempt does not succeed, very little is lost.

Most cuttings contain enough potential growth within themselves to send out new leaves long before actual rooting has taken place. The only way to be certain a cutting is ready to be potted is to examine the buried portion by partially lifting it, very gently, from the sand.

The roots of a cutting remain quite delicate longer than those of a seedling and must be handled more carefully for the first year or so, until they have become thoroughly established.

Planting seeds

Nature has a safeguard that assures the propagation of her plants. Seeds remain dormant until climatic conditions are right for the survival of the sprouted seedlings. Birches, some fruit trees, and oaks, for example, ripen their seeds in the fall. If they were to sprout, their seedlings would freeze to death during the winter months. They therefore remain dormant until spring. Such seeds may be given an artificial resting period, a process called "stratification," by storing them in moist sand in a cold place for at least a month. It is not necessary that they freeze.

A venerable ginkgo, eighty-seven years old.

Other seeds remain dormant because their shells are so impenetrable that moisture cannot reach the embryos until the required number of months have passed. Still others, elms and some maple seeds among them, remain fertile for very short periods after they ripen, often for only a few days.

Unless the grower wishes to make a special study of seeds, learning how best to treat each species would probably require more time than he wishes to give. If the seeds are bought commercially, instructions on preplanting treatment are often included with the packets. Otherwise one must learn by trial and error.

If seeds are large and quite hard, soaking them in a glass of water for a day or two before planting may be all that is necessary. Some large seeds whose shells are thick and glassy to the touch will not germinate for a year or more unless a shallow cut is made on two sides of the outer coating with a knife or small file. Many other seeds may be planted just as they are.

A seed flat, open ground, or an ordinary clay pot may be used. The writer prefers a clay pot, filling it to within two inches of the top with potting soil placed over a layer of gravel to insure good drainage. Another inch of fine soil is sifted over this, and the seeds are

spaced evenly on the surface. More soil is sifted on until fine seeds are barely covered and larger ones are covered by a layer one-quarter to one-half inch thick, depending on the size of the seed. The surface is pressed down firmly and evenly, and the pot is set in water until all the soil is thoroughly wet. A sheet of glass is then laid over the top, and the pot is placed in a shaded, protected spot. Additional water should be given only when the surface shows signs of becoming dry.

When germination occurs, the glass should be removed immediately. This is especially important in the case of conifer seedlings, which are more subject to damping off than are deciduous seedlings.

As it is safer to transplant a little too late rather than too soon, the seedlings should be given plenty of time to develop sturdy root systems. Some species will do this in a few months; pines may take a year or more.

Grafting

The whole principle of grafting is based on a union between the cambium layers of stock and scion. The cambium layer is the thin layer of new and growing tissue just under the bark; the stock is the rooted portion of the tree; and the scion is a shoot that, when grafted to the stock, will form a new top or branch on it.

Both scion and stock may be cut and fitted together in any way at all as long as their cambium layers touch on at least one edge. Preferably they should touch all around. The joint is then tied firmly with raffia and covered with a grafting wax, which will retain moisture until the union is completed. As the cut edges of the two pieces heal, they form calluses composed of loose growths of cells that fuse together and the scion becomes a permanent part of the stock and starts to grow.

The various names such as bark graft, cleft graft, splice graft, tongue graft, side graft, and veneer graft simply designate the manner in which the scion and stock are cut and fitted together. In improving the shapes of bonsai, the tongue and the veneer grafts are the most useful. They leave the least visible scars and can be used for the two most frequent alterations in bonsai culture, that of adding a side branch to a bare space on the trunk and that of combining the top portion of one species with the trunk and root system of another.

The tongue graft is accomplished by cutting both scion and stock on a matching slant. A short perpendicular cut is then made in the cut face of each and the two pieces fitted together as shown.

 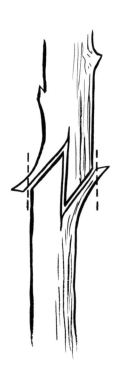

In the veneer graft a wedge is removed from the stock by making a long, slanting cut downward and a shorter cut upward and outward. Both sides of the scion are then cut to fit.

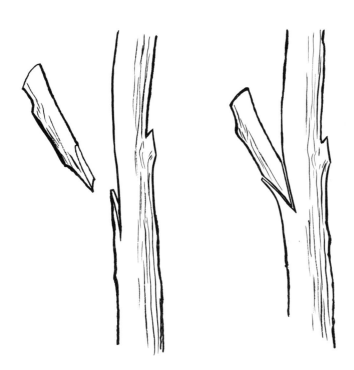

The best time for making these two grafts is in early spring, a little before repotting time, while the plants are still dormant. It is a good idea, when attempting grafting for the first time, to experiment first with full-sized trees. These will not be harmed or noticeably disfigured if early attempts to make matching cuts in stock and scion are not successful. When the technique has been perfected it may then be used on the potted trees without fear of leaving irradicable scars on the bark.

Layering

The simplest method of obtaining a rooted branch by layering is to bend a young, flexible branch over so that it touches the ground about a foot or so from its tip. At this point a slit is made and held open with a pebble. The branch is fastened in place by stakes or wires so it will not move in a strong wind, and earth is mounded over the section containing the slit. When roots have formed in the mound, the rooted branch end is cut from the parent tree or bush and potted. Great care must be taken not to injure the new roots, as they are quite delicate.

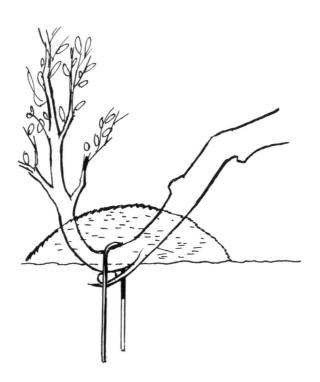

If the branch end to be rooted is too far from the ground to be bent in this way, it may be air-layered. Here the rooting medium is taken to the branch instead of the other way around. The branch is slit as before at the point where roots are desired, and a generous ball of moist sphagnum moss tied around it. The moss is then covered with plastic and tied at both ends. With quick-rooting trees such as willows the moss will probably not dry out before rooting has taken place, but it will have to be watered from time to time with trees that take longer, since it should remain continuously moist.

These two methods will work only on fairly easy-to-root species and on yearling branches. It is almost impossible to root the old, thick branches of most species.

In the third method, which takes longer but promises more chance of success, a young branch is bent to the ground in the same way as in ground layering. After a season has passed, a section of bark is scraped from the buried portion. This will induce suckers to grow from that point. When their stems have partially hardened, a layer of earth two to four inches thick should be mounded over their base. In most cases the suckers will then form roots of their own. When these have become well established, the suckers are removed and another season is allowed to pass before the branch, with attached roots, is removed from the parent plant.

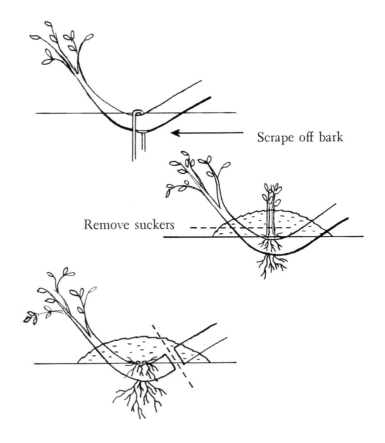

Chapter III

THE FIRST POTTING

The trees to be trained as bonsai have now been bought, found, or propagated, and it is time for their first potting.

This is a good place to pause and learn something about how trees grow, for such knowledge will be invaluable in all the work to come. If the grower understands the interrelationship between roots and branches and leaves, he can make his own bonsai rules, depending on what he wants his trees to do.

There is very little difference between the root systems of all trees. There may be a long or a short tap root or none at all. The side roots may be long or short, the fibrous roots may be many or few. Some trees send their roots a little deeper into the ground than others, but in general root habits and functions are identical in all species.

Contrary to popular belief, the depth of the roots does not correspond exactly to the height of the tree, nor does the length of the side roots match the tree's width. With the exception of the tap root, which has few side roots, most of a tree's roots grow near the surface in the region of the topsoil and often extend far beyond the length of the branches.

However, the shape of the tree will generally correspond to the pattern of the roots. If the roots are evenly spaced around the trunk, the branches will follow the same arrangement. If the roots are sparse and the fibrous roots few, there will be a similar sparsity in the branches. They will be widely spaced and lacking in twiggy growth.

Fibrous roots are simply clusters of very fine roots. They are the result of continual branching and rebranching of the main roots and greatly increase the total root area of a plant. In one study of a single plant of rye, the main roots totaled a length of 214 feet, but the total length of the fibrous roots was nearly 2,000,000 feet.

It is understandable, then, why these fibrous roots are of far more importance in transplanting than are the long, unbranched side roots and why the greater the number that can be moved with the tree, the greater the chances of success. Trees such as the sweetgum, oak and most nut trees, or trees that are in poor condition, have comparatively few fibrous roots and are therefore more difficult to transplant.

Contrary to popular belief also, the tap root is not necessary to the life of the tree. It serves the same general purposes as the other roots; it helps to anchor the tree and does its part in furnishing water and nutrients in liquid form to the above-ground growth. If there are a sufficient number of side roots with attached fibrous roots to do this work alone, the tree can get along very well without its tap root.

Trees vary in their growing periods. All put out new growth in the spring. Some, like pines, may then rest until the following spring, although unusual conditions may cause them to grow again in early fall. Some, including many deciduous trees, grow twice a year, in spring and fall. Some have intermittent growing and resting periods all summer, and some grow steadily during the warm months without resting at all. Suckers do not have growing periods, but grow continuously until a balance with the roots has been regained.

Young potted trees, to be trained as bonsai, are usually allowed to go through as many summer growth periods as is normal for their species, since it is desirable that they increase in size as quickly as possible. It is one of the marks of an expert grower, however, that he allows his mature, fully trained bonsai only one growth period a year. If the roots are crowded to just the right degree, if feedings are held to a minimum, if the mature tree is given as much sunlight as it can stand and just enough water to maintain life, it will not have enough strength to follow its usual growth pattern. This, however, is the ideal of which the beginner should be aware, but which he should not attempt to reach until he has gained more experience.

Finally there is one law of nature that is of far more importance to the bonsai grower than any other, for if he is thoroughly familiar with it he can control the growth of his trees in nearly any way he wishes.

This is the law of supply and demand. Nature established this law long before man recognized its existence in the world of business, and in both cases the principle is very much the same.

The root system and the above-ground portion (which will be referred to as the *top*) of any plant, if allowed to grow unhampered, are in almost perfect functional balance. Under ideal growing conditions the root system supplies as much food and water as the top is able to use, and no more. The top, in turn, demands only enough to maintain a normal rate of growth and a healthy condition.

The growing conditions of very few trees, however, are ideal. Age, soil, insects and disease, cramped growing space, weather extremes (and the bonsai grower with his pruning tools), tend to upset this balance, and the growth pattern changes. How it changes depends on what portion of the tree has been affected.

If the top is injured or cut back, the roots are left for a time with an extra supply of potential growth for which there is no demand. They will then tend to create a new "market" by forcing the top to grow new shoots. If, because of age or some other factor, the top cannot grow enough new shoots to use the extra supply, suckers will appear and grow quickly until the balance has been regained. This explains the presence of the many suckers often seen around the stump of a tree which has been cut down; in this case the demand has suddenly been removed altogether while the supply has remained the same.

If, on the other hand, the root system cannot grow normally, the top must decrease its demands to fit the reduced supply from below. Its growth rate will slow down or stop altogether, sometimes temporarily, sometimes permanently. New leaves and branches may be abnormally small. If the supply has been reduced too much, whole

The Japanese red maple is easy to grow and is one of the best of bonsai subjects.

branches or the entire plant may die. Short of the latter, it is this condition which is ideal for producing dwarfed trees.

If a tree has had an insufficient supply from its root system for years, even though it may have been growing in the open ground, it has the same growth pattern as a pot-bound or root-bound plant. Its branches may become so dried and woody that they will never again be able to produce new growth. In this case, if conditions are improved so that the roots are again able to grow normally, suckers will sprout and take the place of the tree as an outlet for the renewed supply from below. The old trunk and branches may then die. It is important, therefore, not to improve suddenly the growing conditions of a mature bonsai; the tree itself may not be able to use all the fresh supply from the roots, but this supply will be welcomed by unwanted new suckers.

There is one other facet of this supply-and-demand system with which the grower should be familiar. If many new, live roots are cut back without the whole root system having been damaged materially, numerous fresh roots may grow from the cut ends, thus increasing the supply. This may or may not be what the grower intended, for the top will then show a tendency to maintain the balance by putting out corresponding new shoots. In finished bonsai this fresh growth is usually unwanted; in young trees it may be welcome, again depending on the grower's wishes.

The first potting

If any one factor in growing bonsai is of paramount importance for the novice, it is the time chosen for potting. It is an exaggeration, but not a great one, to say that it is impossible to kill any tree by judicious trimming of its roots if it is done at the proper time. The statement comes even closer to the truth in the case of a young deciduous tree.

In early spring, probably March or early April depending on the species and where it has spent the winter, the buds on the branches should be examined. If they show signs of swelling, with just a hint of green at the tips, or if the new, light green needles on conifers are beginning to unfold, the time is right for doing any necessary root work. Repotting and root trimming in early fall, at the start of a new growing period, is perfectly safe for some trees and sometimes preferable with fruit trees that bloom in early spring. But for the beginner, early spring potting is his best insurance against failure.

Procedures for potting the new tree will be discussed in five sections:

> Choosing the container
> Preparing the soil mixture
> Preparing the pot
> Root trimming
> Potting and pruning

CHOOSING THE CONTAINER

The harmony between pot and tree is almost as much a part of bonsai as the tree itself and is covered fully later on. At present, however, shape and color of the container will be disregarded; only size and material are of importance here.

Pots should be as porous as possible. The best material from this standpoint is wood or the coarse clay used in ordinary flowerpots. Because they have superior lasting qualities, however, most bonsai containers are made of ceramic materials, which are harder and somewhat less porous. For the sake of appearance many containers glazed on the outside. Inside they are always left unglazed. Metal, glass, or china containers, or those glazed both inside and out are the least desirable as they absorb no water at all and tend to keep the soil too wet.

All pots, no matter of what size or material, must have at least one drainage hole in the bottom. Large, flat pots should have more. This is one of the few musts in this book, for good drainage is essential in growing potted trees. Containers made especially for bonsai, usually but not always imported, can now be found in most larger cities. In smaller communities, however, the grower may have to order them from catalogues or select simple containers from local florist shops or department stores.

If a container that has all the other desirable qualities lacks proper holes, they can be drilled easily in most materials if an electric hand drill or, preferably, a drill press is available. A pointed carborundum drill point should be used for clay or pottery, and the area being drilled should be kept wet to reduce the heat and lessen the danger of breakage. If a break does occur during drilling, it can be neatly and permanently mended with one of the remarkable epoxy glues. Wood containers can be drilled with a twist drill or auger bit.

The size of the pot selected will depend not only on tree size, but on age, time of year, and what the grower wishes his new tree to do. His situation should fit into one of the following categories, which will then serve as a guide for choosing a container of the right size:

If it is the wrong time of year for planting (after growth has started in spring until early fall), the roots should be disturbed as little as possible. If the tree must be moved, the new pot should be approximately the same size as the old one; or the tree may be planted in open ground until the next season.

A tree whose roots are confined and crowded will grow slowly, so the question of whether to confine roots further by replanting in a smaller container depends on how mature the tree is. The beginner has a tendency to put any tree in its final container immediately, simply because he can't wait to see how it will look. If the trunk is small and uninteresting, however, he will save time in the long run by allowing it to grow for a year or two in an ordinary clay pot, called a "training pot," or he may use the short-cut method described in Chapter IX.

In early spring before growth has started, the roots of most hardy deciduous trees, such as maples, elms, flowering quinces, and willows, to name a few, will stand a great deal of abuse. If the trunk is already of a satisfactory size, a final bonsai pot may be used and the roots trimmed by one-half or more to fit it.

Some easy-to-grow conifers, such as junipers, can stand more root trimming than others. However, conifer roots generally should not be cut back by more than one-third or one-fourth. It may be necessary, therefore, to reduce the size of a conifer root ball gradually, by moving it into a pot of an intermediate size before putting it into its final container the following year.

Juniper.

Sargent juniper found in a neglected field just thirteen months before this picture was taken. Below, as it appeared after digging.

The roots of a naturally dwarfed tree have already been badly disturbed by the first digging and should not be trimmed further until they have had a chance to recover. If a pot is used at all, it should be large enough to take all the roots. Again, this is not a rule, but a safety measure.

If a tree is still young and supple, it is not always possible for the grower to know what its final shape will be. Sometimes an upright tree, for example, will have more *gei* if trained later in a cascade style. It would therefore be wise to allow it to develop its own natural characteristics in a fairly good-sized training pot for a year or more, before deciding on the shape and depth of its final container.

It has been pointed out that a nursery tree growing in a container has been transplanted at least once, and its roots are already partially confined. As a result, its roots can usually be trimmed more severely than would be safe for a natural tree of the same age and species. For this first potting, therefore, a nursery tree can be planted in a somewhat smaller container than would be used for a freshly dug natural tree.

PREPARING THE SOIL MIXTURE

Most bonsai potting mixtures contain the same three ingredients: loam or topsoil, sharp river sand, and a humus of leaf mold or peat moss. As a rule, soil furnishes the growing medium and food for the roots, sand keeps the mixture friable and facilitates drainage, and humus helps to maintain the moisture content and temperature at a fairly uniform level.

Experts usually agree on the contents of the mixture, but less often on the proper proportions. The grower may wish to vary these as he gains in experience, but if he mixes equal portions of the three to start, he will have a good potting soil that will suit the needs of most of his plants.

Sharp sand and topsoil may be purchased almost anywhere, but in many parts of the country leaf mold is difficult, if not impossible, to find. It is a better all-purpose humus than peat moss, as it furnishes a natural food for the plants and is usually less acid. It is good bonsai practice for the grower to make his own leaf mold by storing autumn leaves in a pit. He can speed the decaying process by sprinkling them with a commercial mixture made for the purpose, which may be bought at most nurseries. When the leaves turn black and crumble to the touch, they are ready to use.

If this is impracticable, peat moss may be used with satisfactory results. Although it has no food value at all, it will add the proper texture to the mixture.

Since peat moss is an acid-forming medium, it should be used instead of leaf mold with acid-loving plants, such as azaleas and rhododendrons. Others such as hollies and sorrel trees seem to prefer the acid soil that peat gives, but can be grown satisfactorily in the same mixture used for most other trees.

To avoid large lumps of soil, sticks, stones, or unrotted leaves that may cause air pockets harmful to roots, both the soil and leaf mold should be sifted before they are mixed with the sand. Again, there is disagreement among experienced growers as to what size the sieve holes should be. If the mixture is too coarse, the roots cannot develop properly. If it is too fine, the drainage will be bad.

A principle of good drainage is that the potting material should range from the coarsest at the bottom to the finest on top. Some growers recommend using from three to seven different sieve sizes to obtain these mixtures and discarding all soil that sifts through the finest holes.

The writer's experience indicates, however, that this is not necessary. In wide, shallow pots the drainage will be adequate if there are a number of drainage holes. In moderately deep pots an inch or so of gravel at the bottom is usually enough to facilitate drainage. In deep pots it may or may not be necessary to use several mixtures of varying coarseness; much depends on the shape of the container and the number and size of the roots.

A rule-of-thumb is that the mixture for very small pots should be rather fine, an average-sized tree with many small roots should be given a medium mixture, and one with heavy roots in a larger pot will take a fairly coarse mixture. Three sieves, with four, eight, and twelve or sixteen holes to the linear inch, should be all the grower needs.

If this sounds more formidable than it really is, remember that trees, like all plants, can do quite well under less than ideal conditions. If sieves are not obtainable, the coarse, solid pieces may be picked from the mixture by hand, and the rest crumbled to an even consistency with the fingers.

PREPARING THE POT

Each drainage hole should first be covered with a stone, a broken piece of clay pot, or a square of plastic screening. Next, in any but shallow containers, about an inch of gravel should be added, then another inch or so of potting mixture (of the coarsest size, if more than one is to be used). The pot is then ready for planting.

Root trimming

Trimming the roots for this first planting is simple; cut off only enough to allow the tree to fit into its new pot. If this can be done without cutting any roots at all, they should be left untouched.

The tree is taken from its container and the size of its root ball reduced by picking the soil away with a pointed stick, carefully, so that the roots will not be damaged. When the root ball is about an inch smaller all around than the space inside the prepared pot, the exposed roots are cut off with sharp scissors. The root ball should then be held inside the container and measured for depth. If its top is more than one-and-a-half inches below the top edge of any but a very shallow pot, more soil should be added to the bottom to raise it to the proper level. If the container is shallow, for this first potting it is often necessary that the top of the root ball be level with or even extend above the top edge of the pot. The tree may then be lowered gradually to the desired depth during subsequent repottings.

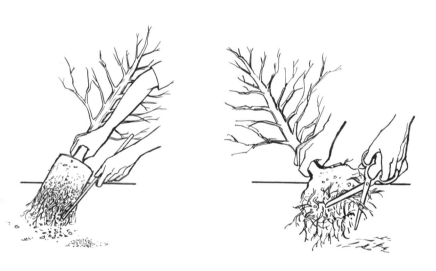

When a tree has been growing in a deep container, and its roots must be spread to fit into a shallow one, more than the usual amount of soil must be removed. If so, it is less damaging to the root system if the soil is not picked off dry, but washed away with a gentle stream of water. The roots are then spread flat and the ends trimmed where necessary.

POTTING AND PRUNING

With the tree in place, the pot is next filled with the soil mixture, which is worked down thoroughly with the stick until there is little chance that any air pockets remain around the roots. More soil is added and worked down as before until the pot is nearly full. A space of one-half to one inch should be left at the top for watering. Next, this space is filled with water, as many times as necessary, until moisture can be seen coming from the drainage holes at the bottom.

In order to help the tree maintain its supply-and-demand balance, light pruning should be done at this time. Very long branches should be cut back, and those that will obviously not add to the *gei* of the tree when it receives its final shaping should be removed entirely.

All that remains to be done to establish the tree in its new home is to keep it shaded and protected from strong winds for a few weeks until new growth shows it is alive and growing well. It may then be moved gradually into sunlight, with an hour or two of additional exposure each day.

From this point until it needs repotting, the tree needs only the normal, day-to-day care of any potted plant. It should be watered, fed, and protected from weather extremes and insects. Its shape and appearance will gradually be improved by wiring and pruning.

Once he has potted his trees, the grower will find himself paying them frequent, unnecessary visits. If he is wise, he will realize that they need his constant companionship far less than he needs theirs; for it is from this point that the real pleasure of growing bonsai begins.

Chapter IV

WATERING

A WATERING schedule can no more be followed for bonsai than it can for a lawn. In both instances the season, humidity, sunlight, and temperature all determine how quickly water in the soil will evaporate and need replacing. In addition, some trees, such as willows and firs, need more water than others; trees whose roots have crowded most of the soil from their pots will dry more quickly than newly potted ones.

The soil in bonsai pots, as it is with most potted plants, should never be allowed to dry out completely, nor should it be kept constantly wet. It is a law of nature that roots always grow toward moisture, and leaves and branches always grow toward light. An occasional soaking, therefore, is preferable to many light waterings of the soil surface, since a thorough wetting encourages the roots to grow deep into the pot where a maximum of growing space and nutrients is available to them. Light watering encourages the growth of roots toward the surface, where they are more subject to injury and to drying out between waterings.

The ideal method is to set the pots in water and allow it to rise through the drainage holes until the surface of the soil is dark and moist. However, when there are many trees this method is so time-consuming that few growers practice it regularly except where roots have filled a pot to the brim. In this case, until the tree is repotted and its roots trimmed, watering from below is the most efficient method.

If, to save time, a tree is watered on the surface, the space at the top of the pot should be filled as many times as necessary, until water drips from the drainage holes.

In cool weather, it is better to water too little than too much, if there must be a choice. During the hot, dry, weather of midsummer, however, it is next to impossible to overwater a tree if the drainage in the pot is good.

During the active growing season of spring and early summer, the amount of water one gives depends to a great extent on what he wants the trees to do. Generous watering during this period encourages rapid growth. A young tree whose finished shape has not yet been determined will therefore increase in trunk size more quickly if it is given enough water, while a mature bonsai should be watered sparingly, to produce a minimum of growth.

Some experienced growers recommend that during this period a bonsai be allowed to become quite dry, to the point where a deciduous tree will wilt, before additional water is given. The novice would do well to avoid this practice until he has become thoroughly familiar with his plants. Though a deciduous tree may give immediate warning when it has become too dry and may revive quickly when watered again, in hot weather a delay of just an hour or two after wilting can do permanent harm. A conifer does not show wilt, as is evidenced by the length of time a Christmas tree will stay fresh and green after its roots have been removed; so it is dangerous for the beginner to try to stunt its growth in this way. The results of injury to most conifers, especially pines, from lack of water in the spring may not show up until fall, when the needles may lose color and start to drop. By then it is often too late to save the tree.

As the days grow shorter and cooler, less water is needed. Watering should not be neglected altogether in cold weather, however, for winter air with its low humidity can be very drying to any plant.

Once or twice a week should take care of the average tree, and the soil does not need to be soaked as thoroughly as it does in summer.

In extremely cold areas, where the temperature drops well below freezing and stays there for long periods, watering should be omitted as long as the soil in the pots remains frozen.

Whether one uses a watering can or a hose, a gentle spray is best for the trees. A stream of water should never be of such force as to disturb the surface soil in the pots.

An occasional spraying of the bonsai leaves is important, particularly in the city, where the air is not always clean. In hot weather this should be done in early evening, after the sun has set, in order to avoid leaf burn. If the trees are growing under a lath screen there is also the possibility that rainfall, after a long dry spell, will wash accumulated dirt from the slats down onto the trees. When this dries it can form an impenetrable barrier between the leaves and the air they must have. It is therefore good practice to spray trees immediately after such a rain.

Much has been written about rain water versus tap water for bonsai. For many city growers this becomes another academic question since they have no facilities for collecting rain water. Often the very suggestion that this is necessary is enough to frighten them away from growing bonsai altogether.

Rain water is soft; it soaks into the soil at air temperature and feeds the roots with nutrients it has picked up from the atmosphere. City tap water usually contains some chemicals, but the writer has used it for many years and has observed no ill effects on the trees.

As to temperature, in cool weather tap water is cool; in hot weather it is comparatively warm. It is not as warm as the air, but any gardener who has thirsted for a drink of cold water and taken it from the hose knows there was not as much difference between water and air temperatures as he would have liked. In the writer's opinion, potted trees are made of much sterner stuff than they are often given credit for, and this question of water temperature matching air temperature has more importance in theory than in practice.

The amount of nutrients the trees miss when tap water is used instead of rain water is slight and can be made up for very easily by occasional feedings. Where the water, whether from a well or city reservoir, has a high mineral content and is quite hard, the grower would be wise to collect rain water for his trees. If, however, he has been able to use such water satisfactorily on other potted plants, it should also be usable for bonsai.

Chapter V

FEEDING

THERE are almost as many recommendations on feeding bonsai as there are experts to make them. Suggested schedules range from weekly summer feedings to no food at all. The disagreement on this point should give the beginner a sense of security, for no matter what reasonable amount of food he gives his trees, there is probably an experienced grower somewhere following much the same routine.

For the most part, those who omit food entirely are Japanese with a lifetime of experience, who are caring for mature bonsai from fifty to several hundred years old. In feeding such trees one must strike a delicate balance between giving just enough to maintain life but not enough to force new growth. Since their great skill enables them to keep these trees alive without any food at all, the grower with less skill can only envy them as he reaches for the fertilizer: It should be added, however, that other Japanese growers with equally good reputations feed their trees regularlyl.

WHAT TO FEED

Although some foods used extensively for bonsai are difficult to find in the average nursery, there are so many to choose from that the grower should be able to find at least one. Here are some:

Soybean meal	Cottonseed meal
Fish meal	Bone meal
Fish emulsion	Rapeseed meal
Barnyard manures	Chicken meal

In addition, there are balanced, commercial plant foods containing mixtures of bone meal, dried blood, ground fish, etc. The writer regularly uses one of these. They are packaged under various trade names and give excellent results.

The only restriction is that the food should be a natural one. Chemical fertilizers are too strong and act too quickly for bonsai.

How much to feed

More important by far than what or when to feed is the question of how much to feed. A short discussion of the purposes and results of feeding bonsai should enable the reader to decide for himself what will be best for his own trees.

In some respects a young tree is much like an active child, and nature's system of supply and demand applies to each. The appetite of a normal child enables him to eat not only enough food to maintain his daily health, but an additional amount to "grow on." After he reaches maturity the demands of his body decrease, and if the supply is not decreased accordingly, the extra food he no longer needs for growth will be stored in his body as fat.

Obviously a tree does not store fat, but the principle of its growth is similar to that of the child's. When young and growing rapidly, its demand on the root system is greater than it will be in future years. A small amount of extra food will result in a more rapid increase in height and trunk size. As the tree grows older and its branches and trunk become woody, its growth rate slows down and its demand for food decreases in the same degree. From then on, excess food is apt to result in spurts of bushy growth, large leaves or long needles, or suckers.

If an overfed tree is still relatively young and has not yet been trained as a bonsai, such results are not too serious; the grower has at least learned how much *not* to feed his tree, and the mistake can be rectified in future years by pruning and shaping. If, however, the tree is a mature bonsai, its appearance can be spoiled by such over-feeding. Years of effort spent in bringing it to near-perfection will have been wasted, for the work will have to be done over again.

Results of overfeeding a dwarfed pine. Scattered needles have reverted to normal length.

Food is given to bonsai in one of three forms: dry, paste, and liquid. Each has an advantage over the others. The only dis-advantage of paste and liquid forms is the preliminary work re-quired in preparing them.

DRY FORM

This is the simplest of the three to use. Granular or powdered food is sprinkled evenly over the soil and watered in. It is impossible to state the exact amount to be used, because species, age, pot size and strength of the food chosen must all be considered. As a rule, enough food to give the soil a gray, dusty appearance is about right.

PASTE FORM

Various meals, such as rapeseed or cottonseed, are often given in the form of a paste. The dry food is mixed with a small amount of water and allowed to stand in a closed jar for a few weeks until a thick paste is formed. This is shaped into balls about the size of small marbles. From three to six of these are placed around the edge of the soil of an average pot. There are two advantages to this method: the food is absorbed slowly as the tree is watered, and the balls will adhere to the sloping sides of soil that has been mounded in the pot.

LIQUID FORM

This is the form most used with manures. One part of the manure is combined in a closed container with ten parts of water. The mixture should be stirred every few days for a period of a month or so in warm weather, or two or three months in winter. The liquid is then drained off and stored in jars, and the solids at the bottom are discarded. Diluted with water, this liquid is given to the tree in about the same amount as would be given in a single watering.

Disagreement again appears among experienced growers as to what degree of dilution is advisable. Since the recommendations vary from ten parts to as much as thirty parts of water for each part of the liquid manure, the novice would be wise to start with the weakest solution. It will then be safe to give two or three additional feedings during the summer if they seem advisable.

No matter in what form fertilizer is used, it is always best that the soil be damp at the time of feeding. This eliminates the possibility that the food will burn the roots.

Learning how much to feed a tree is not difficult; it is only necessary to feed sparingly and watch the results. If the young tree grows well and the older one maintains good color without producing unwanted growth, the right amount is being used for each. If it is insufficient, it can easily by increased; but if it is excessive, it cannot be withdrawn. Very small feedings at the start are therefore indicated, and it will probably be found that these will be adequate.

WHEN TO FEED

Two feedings a year, in spring and early fall, should be enough for most trees. Trees with spring bloom, such as fruit trees or wistaria, will appreciate an extra feeding in the fall, just before their dormant periods. Very small trees in miniature pots need to be fed more often, because they are growing in such a small amount of soil.

Fresh soil mixture contains enough natural food to sustain the average tree for about a year. If, for some special reason, the grower wishes to feed a newly repotted tree, he should wait at least a month for it to become established before doing so.

It should be remembered that plant food is a steak dinner, not a medicine, and should be given only to a good, healthy tree; it is more apt to kill than cure one that is sickly or diseased.

Because a tree puts out most of its year's growth in the spring, food at this time will give such growth an added push. In young trees where this is desirable, spring and fall feedings should be of equal size. An older tree, however, should have a very light feeding in spring and a heavier one in fall. This will supply the necessary nutrients without producing unwanted new shoots.

As with most instructions which must be given in print, the problem of feeding is much less complicated than it may appear to be. If the beginner wishes to omit fertilizer altogether for the first year or two, he may do so. No appreciable harm will have been done. Where feeding bonsai is concerned, nature forgives the sin of omission much more readily than she does that of overcommission.

With its pink blossoms in early spring and bright, appropriately small fruit in summer, the flowering crab makes an excellent bonsai subject.

Chapter VI

SUMMER AND WINTER PROTECTION

Bonsai should not be pampered where protection from the elements is concerned. As a whole, the basic needs of each species remains the same, whether in a forest or a small container. A subtropical tree must be given full protection in cold climates; it does not follow that a hardy, deciduous tree will appreciate, or even survive, the same treatment.

In discussing the weather of various parts of the country the same words can mean many different things. The full sun, often recommended for dwarfed trees in books, is one thing in Texas, another in New York, and still another in Oregon. The snows and freezing cold of Arkansas are not the same as those of Idaho, Michigan, or even Missouri.

Generalities are therefore of little help. Instead, it will be better to discuss protection in the hottest and coldest parts of the country. The reader can then place himself according to the area in which he lives and use his best judgment to determine how much protection his own trees will need.

Summer protection

Because it is the easy way, too many bonsai growers tend to keep their trees in shade or half-shade. This often does no harm to the trees. They may grow lush, green, tall, and attractive, but they are not bonsai.

As every gardener knows, if two identical sun-loving plants are grown, one in shade and the other in full sun, they will soon look entirely different. The sun-grown plant will be shorter, broader, more sturdy; its leaves will be smaller, its blooms more numerous.

Since these are all qualities desirable for bonsai, a potted tree of a species that prefers full sun should be given all it can stand. Half-shade should be given only to a tree, such as a fir, that normally requires it.

Bonsai, however, cannot tolerate quite as much sun as full-sized trees of the same species. Their roots cannot go deep into the soil for protection, their pots become overheated, and in hot climates it is almost impossible to keep the moisture content of the soil at the even level most trees prefer. Therefore if the midsummer sun is scorching, the humidity low, and the temperature high, nearly all trees will require some shade.

Fortunately before permanent harm is done, the grower usually has warning that a tree is receiving too much sun. Needles of coni-fers lose color; deciduous leaves turn brown and crisp at the edges and tender new leaves and shoots may dry altogether and drop off. The tree begins to take on a generally unhealthy appearance.

Protection from the sun can be given in several ways. If there are only a few trees, they can be kept on a bench under a tall tree, where the sunlight is dappled. They can be placed on the east side of a fence or shrubbery border, where they will receive only the morning sun. Best of all, they can be grown in a small lath house. If there are many trees to be protected building such a house will be well worth the effort.

The slats of a lath house for bonsai should not be spaced as close together as are the slats of most nursery lath houses, where slats and spaces are approximately equal in width. This reduces the sunlight by about one-half. Even in areas where there is constant, burning sunlight, slats one-half the width of the spaces should give enough protection for potted trees. They should always run in a north-south direction so that the strips of light on the trees will move as the sun progresses from east to west.

Weather-resistant wood is the material most used for slats, but aluminum stripping has many advantages. It is lightweight, weather-proof, needs no paint, and comes in attractive shades of green that blend well with the trees. It can be purchased in large rolls from Venetian blind companies and cut as desired.

Two views of a lath screen built especially for bonsai.

Although a potted tree may safely be moved from sun to shade in one step, the reverse is not true. It can be killed easily if it has been growing in shade and is given abrupt, full sunlight for a prolonged period. The tree should be moved into the sun gradually, an additional hour or two each day.

Dwarfed trees grown close to a building may be damaged by reflected heat from the wall. They should be placed far enough away so its heat cannot reach them.

Pots should be spaced far enough apart for air to circulate freely between them.

If bonsai are kept on the ground they are more readily accessible to insects. Though not necessary, it is a good idea to use wooden benches of a convenient height.

Winter protection

Although too much summer sun is not often fatal to bonsai, the same cannot be said of snow, ice, and sudden, extreme changes in winter temperature. These can cause irreparable damage.

Again, experts disagree on what particular element is responsible for the trouble caused by winter weather. Blame has been placed on frost; drying winds; freezing and thawing of the soil; too much cold moisture, which may cause root-rot; or the expansion of frozen soil, which may cause the pots to break, thus exposing the roots to winter air. Naming the culprit, however, is unimportant. With proper protection all will be rendered harmless.

The one point of agreement is that low temperatures will not hurt a hardy tree. On the contrary, if such a tree is kept warm all winter it cannot go into dormancy and rest and will gradually weaken and die.

Any location, then, where hardy trees remain cold and protected from uncontrolled moisture is ideal. Building a frame over a bench and covering it with plastic or burlap is recommended by some growers. One end should be left open for ventilation. In some climates this covered-bench method is satisfactory. In others, sturdy as the arrangement may seem in November, it may prove no match for the whipping winds and heavy snows of January or February.

Several winters of trial and error plus a generous heap of small, dead trees have convinced the writer that the safest place for hardy bonsai in severe climates is a well-ventilated, unheated room. This may be an enclosed porch, a basement room, or a separate building such as a shed. An open porch or breezeway is also satisfactory if the trees are placed close to the house, away from snow and rain that may blow in. Apartment dwellers have had success in wintering their trees on roofed fire escapes by placing them in wooden crates turned on their sides, with the openings facing the building.

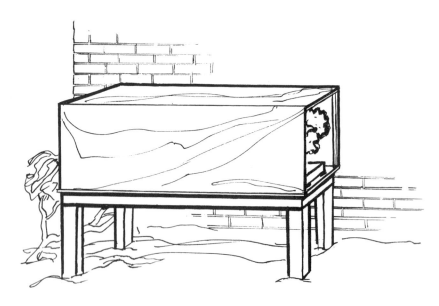

Tropical and subtropical trees must be wintered under glass in cold areas. Trees listed as hardy, but of doubtful hardiness in severe climates, may also be wintered under glass in these areas, but the temperature should be kept as close to the minimum level of safety as possible. No matter how hardy their species, young trees up to a year old should be given extra protection in winter.

Since deciduous trees have no leaves when dormant, whether or not they receive light during the winter is unimportant. Conifers and broad-leaved evergreens, however, hold their foliage all year and need light to maintain good color. They should be placed near a window, out of the direct sun, to receive as much winter light as possible.

In very mild sections, where an occasional below-freezing temperature is a phenomenon, most hardy trees and shrubs cannot be grown successfully. This should be no drawback, for there are many beautiful trees native to each area which, when dwarfed, can well prove to be the envy of growers in more severe climates. Such trees also have the advantage of seldom needing any winter protection.

Some growers have had success wintering a few dwarfed plants such as box, ivy, and citrus fruits indoors. But as a rule no bonsai should be kept in the house, winter or summer, for long periods. They may be brought in for display, but should be rotated so that none spends more than a few days at a time indoors.

Chapter VII

INSECTS AND SICK TREES

In theory, insects do not bother the bonsai that is well watered, fed, and ventilated. In theory, also, most of them can be eliminated if they are washed from the leaves and stems with water.

Unfortunately, insects do appear occasionally on healthy bonsai just as they do on any other plant. And though washing them off is sometimes good practice, it has one shortcoming: they tend to come back, wet but still hungry.

Because bonsai are more susceptible to injury from strong poison sprays than are full-sized trees, the most gentle treatment that will effectively rid them of pests is the one to use. If trees are watched carefully, the first few insects to appear can usually be discovered before serious infestation occurs. They can then be controlled without a general spraying.

If there are just a few chewing insects, for example, they can be picked off by hand and destroyed.

The waxy shells of certain insects, such as mealy bugs, are impervious to poison sprays with a water base. An oil emulsion will usually control them; but if there are not too many, other methods are easier on the tree. They may be picked from the plant with a cotton-tipped stick dipped in alcohol, which will penetrate their shells and kill them. Because of its drying quality, care should be taken not to get too much alcohol on the tree itself.

If insects are too numerous for this method or if they are clustered in the needles of a conifer and cannot be reached, covering the tree thickly with a lather made by whisking a detergent and tepid water together briskly is often effective. The suds are allowed to stand on the tree for ten minutes, then are washed off with a gentle spray. The soil should first be protected with a sheet of plastic tied snugly to the trunk to prevent the detergent from reaching the roots.

If needles or whole branches of conifers turn brown, red spiders may be attacking the tree. Less than one-sixtieth of an inch in length, they are difficult to see; but if the branch is held over a sheet of white paper and shaken vigorously, some of the tiny insects will drop off and become visible on the paper. Red spiders seldom attack a tree around which there is free circulation of air, or a tree that is exposed to occasional good, stiff breezes. Washing them off with a spray from the hose is the simplest control, but this must be repeated weekly during the summer or they will reappear. Fine sulphur dust, a diluted lime-sulphur solution, nicotine sulfate, or rotenone are sprays that will usually hold red spiders in check.

Ants on a tree do little harm in themselves but may attract aphids or carry mealy bugs from one tree to another. Spraying the ground around the benches with an aerosol insect bomb will help to control not only ants, but other crawling insects that may later attack the trees.

Aphids are not difficult to control. If there are just a few, they may be taken off by hand. Nicotine sulfate, rotenone, pyrethrum, or one of the commercial sprays are all effective.

Scale, like aphids, are sucking insects that can be controlled with a nicotine or dormant oil spray. If they are clustered thickly, it is helpful before spraying to remove as many as possible by scraping the stem with a stick or the dull side of a knife blade.

Fungus diseases such as rust, leaf spot, wilt, and mildew can usually be controlled by the reliable old fungicide, Bordeaux mixture, or by a commercial spray made for the purpose.

If poison sprays must be resorted to, and sometimes they must, they should be used only on cloudy, cool days, and sparingly. The labels should be read carefully, and no more than the minimum treatment recommended by the manufacturer should be given at first. If this is not effective and the tree shows no signs of damage, the amount may be increased for the next spraying.

Sick trees

The tree that sickens under the grower's care is telling him, as plainly as it can, that it is hungry for something it is not receiving. It may be asking for more or less water; more growing room for its roots; colder weather during its dormant period; better protection from insects; more or less sunlight, humidity, food, or clean air. Even the simplest philodendron that dies on the kitchen window sill has a story to tell if someone will take the time to listen. There is no such thing as a difficult plant to grow once its needs are understood. Occasionally a potted tree will turn brown and die for no apparent reason. The reason exists, however. If it can be found, a similar occurrence may be avoided in the future.

The basic requirements of trees in general can be learned from books, but the particular needs of each individual bonsai can only be learned from close observation over a long period of time. Fortunately this is an easy task, for no one who grows bonsai can stay away from them for long. And as the grower looks, he learns.

The elm that yesterday was rich and green, today seems different somehow. Is something wrong, or is it just imagination? Do those yellow leaves on the lower branches mean trouble? Perhaps tomorrow will tell. The leaves of the Japanese maple are purple-green, not as red as they should be at this time of year. Let's move it into a sunnier position for a while. There is a thin, dark crust on the dry soil of the Japanese black pine. Was there a period of overwatering in the past or is the drainage poor? We'll watch it when next we water and see. Good news: almost overnight, it seems, the pomegranate is full of flower buds, hard and round, like tiny green beads. We must remember to turn the pot occasionally so they will all be open at the same time. And here is an almost invisible cluster of insects on a new shoot of the persimmon. Aphids. Are there any others on the plant? No. Well, the shoot is unwanted anyway, so we'll remove it now, insects and all, and crush it thoroughly underfoot.

Only in this way can the eyes learn to see. Once they have learned, trouble can be spotted and dealt with in most cases before it becomes serious.

If it does become serious, however, and the tree, whether from causes known or unrecognized, seems to be very sick, there is still hope that it can be saved. Deciduous trees often respond quickly to emergency treatment, most conifers about half of the time, pines almost never.

When a number of trees are being grown, a hospital or "sick bed" in a shaded corner of the garden can be very useful. Room in which to plant two or three trees should be sufficient. If this is not practicable, the sick tree may be planted in a large pot instead.

The conditions in the hospital should be the same as those in a cutting bed: full shade, protection from wind, even moisture, a growing medium of sand or a very light, sandy soil, high humidity, and a constant temperature. The latter is supplied as closely as possible by the shade and protected location. If the humidity is low, a plastic bag from the dry cleaner's can be supported by stakes and placed around the tree.

If it is early spring, the soil may be washed gently from the roots of the sick tree before it is planted in the sand. Later in the summer roots should be disturbed as little as possible and the whole ball buried in the bed just as it is.

Treatment of the tree varies with the reason for which it has been hospitalized. If the roots have been cut very short, the top should be pruned accordingly to restore the supply-and-demand balance. Branches should be cut back or thinned, and it is often helpful to remove most of the leaves. If the roots have not been cut and the tree simply looks bad, above-ground growth should not be disturbed. Like a cutting, the tree may show new growth before roots have started to mend; so all top growth, including suckers, should be left untouched for at least a full season. When such a tree has again been potted, pruning should be delayed until it shows signs that its roots are continuing their recovery.

A year in the hospital is a good place for a newly dug, naturally dwarfed tree or one whose roots have been trimmed so severely the grower has doubts about its chances for survival. A tree whose roots have become so crowded its health is affected may be planted in the bed temporarily, until the proper repotting season. Those that show signs in spring of having received insufficient winter protection often benefit by a growing season in the hospital. Overwatered trees may be saved in this way. If undetected root injury has occurred, a tree can sometimes be brought back to health in the hospital.

The sick-bed method is successful often enough to make it well worth trying, especially if the tree is one of the grower's favorites. If it dies in spite of his efforts, he will know he has done everything possible to save it; he can only take steps to avoid in the future the conditions that may have caused the trouble.

Chapter VIII

REPOTTING AND FUTURE CARE

It is early spring again. The trees that were selected and potted a year ago have changed in size and shape. They are a little taller now, trunks of young trees are noticeably thicker, and there are many more small twigs on the branches of the still leafless deciduous trees.

Some trees that have been in training pots for the past twelve months are ready to be moved into bonsai containers. Others will be allowed to increase in size in their present containers for another year or two. The roots of some still have plenty of room and will need no attention, while others are crowded and hungry for fresh soil. Now, and every spring hereafter, is the time to check to see which of the trees should be repotted.

On the whole, procedures for repotting are the same as they were for the first potting. The same soil mixture is used, and it is again pushed carefully around the roots with a stick, to eliminate air pockets. As before, the tree is watered thoroughly and protected from sun and wind until it has become established.

There has been time this past year for the grower to become acquainted with his trees. He may now wish to repot a tree for any of these five reasons:

To relieve crowded roots

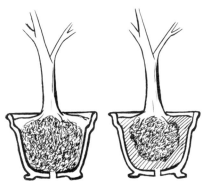

To decrease pot size

To increase pot size

To transplant to a bonsai pot

To improve drainage

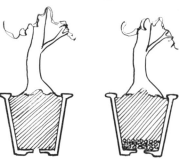

CROWDED ROOTS

Since root trimming and repotting must be continued throughout the life of a bonsai, it is important to understand thoroughly the reasons for doing it and the ways in which it may be done.

"You cut back the roots, don't you?" is the one question the grower will hear over and over again from visitors. The answer to this is "Yes," but the answer to the implied assumption that some mysterious root-trimming method is solely responsible for the size of the tree is "No."

Bonsai roots are trimmed primarily because they have become so crowded in the pot there is no space left for sufficient soil to nourish them and keep them alive. When a houseplant reaches this stage, as it will eventually, the grower simply moves it to a larger pot and adds fresh soil. It will then continue to grow and increase in size at its normal rate.

Part of the art of bonsai, however, is discouraging a mature tree from increasing in size. It must therefore spend its whole lifetime in one container selected to harmonize with its size, shape, and color. As the roots continue to grow, something must give; and since a larger pot cannot be substituted without changing the character of the tree, there is no choice but to decrease the root ball.

The supply-and-demand balance of a naturally dwarfed tree is never disturbed. There is no one to trim its roots, which may be wedged between rocks or crowded among the stronger roots of a larger tree, yet it goes on living for a hundred years or more, its beauty unmarred by sudden new spurts of growth, suckers, or full-sized leaves. If the grower could keep his trees alive in this way, without touching their roots, many of his problems would be solved; but he cannot. This is one of the most misunderstood phases in the dwarfing of trees. The best the grower can do is to allow the confined roots of a mature bonsai to enlarge until its life is endangered. Then he must cut them back, as carefully and selectively as possible.

Roominess of the pot has a much greater influence on eventual size than cutting back the roots. The picture on this page illustrates this point. The two pomegranate trees shown were started from seed at the same time and grown side by side for six months under the same conditions. Then one was planted in a seven-inch pot, the other in a three-inch pot. Their roots were trimmed twice, at the same times. After four years each is a partially dwarfed tree, and the difference in their size is caused solely by the difference in the space allowed for their roots.

How often a tree must be repotted depends on age, growing conditions, pot size, and species. The usual rules, therefore, of repotting a flowering or fruiting tree every year, a deciduous tree every two or three years, and a conifer every three to five years are of little practical value.

The roots of some species, such as crape myrtle and weeping willow, fill the pot more quickly than others. Such trees may have to be repotted twice a year, in spring and early fall. Though the roots of conifers usually grow more slowly than do those of deciduous trees, age is so important in growth rate that a young juniper, for example, may have to be repotted more often than an older maple or elm tree. A fairly large tree will probably have to be repotted more often than a smaller one in a container of the same size.

Therefore, the only way to decide whether or not roots are overcrowded is to look at them and see.

This does not have to be done every year with every tree. As the grower becomes familiar with his own plants he will know that the cryptomeria he planted last spring in an eight-inch pot could not possibly need repotting for another year or two. It is probable, however, that the trident maple he is training as a *mame*, or miniature, bonsai in a two-inch container will need repotting this year and next as well.

In early spring, just as the buds are beginning to swell, the doubtful tree should be taken from its container and its roots examined. If they wind around solidly to follow the shape of the pot with little or no soil showing between them, it is time for repotting. If there is enough soil left along the sides of the root ball to crumble and fall away loosely, the tree may safely be left for another year or two.

The procedure for exposing the roots of the tree to be repotted is the same as it was for the original potting; about one-third of the soil is picked off evenly all around, leaving the roots protruding.

At this point the grower has a choice. If he wishes to simplify his work, he may cut off all the exposed roots, almost to the edge of the soil ball. This indiscriminate root trimming is commonly practiced.

With species whose old roots are not readily distinguishable from the new, it is the easiest way.

The new, live roots of some species, however, are fresh and white and can be seen clearly. Under nature's system of supply and demand, live roots, when cut, tend to branch and cause similar branching of top growth. Keeping this in mind, the grower may prefer to practice selective trimming. He may want to cut away only the dark, dead roots of a mature bonsai, for example, so that its normal balance will be maintained and its finished shape will not be altered by unwanted new shoots. If, on the other hand, he wishes to encourage bushiness in a young deciduous tree, he may trim both the live roots and the branches. This, too, will allow the tree to maintain its balance but will encourage the appearance of additional young branches.

Trimming live roots but not branches will leave the tree with more demand than supply, and new growth will be slowed. But just as the new root growth will tend to branch, so will the new top growth when it does appear.

Selective root trimming gives the grower a chance to influence the new growth of his tree in almost any way he wishes. If he understands thoroughly the principles of supply and demand, logic and not rules will be the only guide he needs.

No matter which trimming method is used, the new root ball should not occupy more than two-thirds to three-fourths of the space in the pot. Fresh soil will fill the rest.

DECREASING POT SIZE

A tree whose root ball is so large at the start it cannot safely be reduced in one step to the size of its final container may be moved to a smaller pot each planting season. One intermediate step is usually all that is necessary, but the number of roots that may be cut off at one time depends on the age and species of the tree. The older the tree, the more sensitive it is to having its roots disturbed.

The roots of a deciduous tree may be cut back drastically in early spring before leaves appear, but a pine of the same age should have no more than the usual one-third or one-fourth of its roots removed at one time. Some other conifers, such as junipers, may be cut back more than this, but if the grower does not know the resistance to abuse of a particular species, it is better to be safe and reduce the root ball slowly.

Root ball of this Swiss stone pine was reduced to less than one third of its original size in two years.

INCREASING POT SIZE

A seedling or a tree whose trunk is still thin and unattractive should be given sufficient room in which to grow freely. If its roots have filled the pot in which it was planted last spring, it should be moved to a slightly larger one. Additional growing room should be provided each time the roots threaten to become crowded. When the tree has reached a desired size, roots may then be cut back to fit a bonsai container.

This Italian stone pine, originally a nursery tree, has been trained for about seven years.

TRANSPLANTING TO A BONSAI POT

If the final container selected is narrower, but of approximately the same depth as the training pot, there will be little trouble in transplanting the tree. If, however, the new container is wide and shallow, most of the soil—and sometimes all of it—will have to be removed from the roots. This may be done carefully with a pointed stick; but if the soil does not crumble easily, there is less chance of injury if it is washed off with a gentle stream of water. The roots can then be spread to fit the new pot and their ends trimmed as necessary.

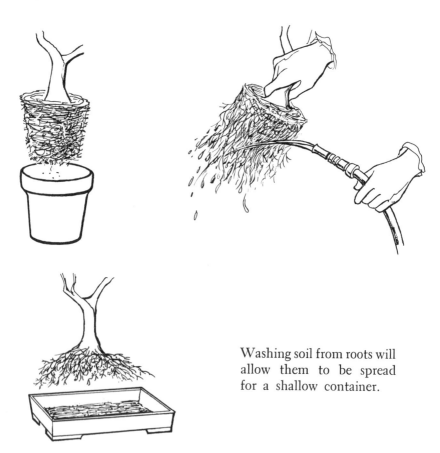

Washing soil from roots will allow them to be spread for a shallow container.

A tree with no soil on its roots is usually top-heavy, and the chances are it will not remain in position in a shallow pot while soil is being added. Until the roots have started to grow in their new, flat shape, they will also have a tendency to be springy and push the tree upward. It is usually necessary, therefore, to tie or wire the tree in place before soil is added. This may be done by fastening a cord or wire to the base of the trunk, bringing the ends through the drainage holes and tying them beneath the pot; or the cord may be fastened to the trunk just above the lowest branches, brought over the ends of the pot and tied beneath.

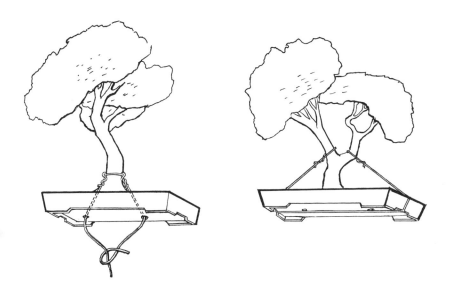

In some cases the bottom roots have been trimmed to the limit of safety but they are still too thick to allow the tree to sit as low in a shallow pot as the grower would like. The tree may be planted as it is, with a mound of soil protruding above the container. The mound should then be covered with moss to prevent its being washed down during watering. The roots can be trimmed a little more each time, until the root ball is as shallow as its container.

One of the most common problems encountered when potting a fairly large tree in a shallow pot is a very thick, stiff root whose angle does not permit the tree to stand erect. This can be solved in several ways. It would be easy, of course, to cut the root off; but if most of the fibrous roots are attached to it, the tree might not survive its complete removal. The safest solution is to shorten the root a little and replant the tree in its former, deep pot. As new fibrous roots develop closer to the trunk, the process can be repeated until the troublesome root is short enough to fit into the shallow container.

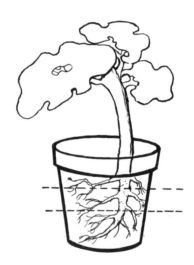

A timesaving but more risky method is to cut part way through the root at the point where a sharp bend is needed. The root is then bent, very slowly and carefully, to the desired angle. The danger is, of course, that there will be a complete break. If this happens, the grower should plant the tree immediately in the sick bed and hope for the best. This partial-cutting method can work very well, but it is not recommended if the tree is highly valued.

If the root is not too stiff, a third method may be used. One end of a length of heavy, rustproof wire is looped around the base of the trunk and coiled around the root all the way to the tip. It may then be bent as much as necessary. Care should be taken not to injure the fibrous roots, and the work should be done quickly so that they will not dry out. The wire may be removed during the next repotting by snipping it in several places with a wire cutter and slipping the pieces out.

IMPROVING DRAINAGE

This first year the trees have been watered often. The grower now knows in which pots the moisture will run quickly through the soil and out the drainage holes as it should, and which will hold water for some time before allowing it to soak in.

Early spring is a good time to improve drainage conditions. Before this is done, however, it is helpful to learn what caused the trouble in the first place. Here are a few of the most common causes of drainage problems, and their cures:

When first acquired, the tree was growing in yellow clay or other poor soil. As a precautionary measure a generous ball of it was left around the roots for the first year. This caused the water to seek the outer edges of the pot, where the soil was more porous. The correction is simple: it is now safe to wash most of the old soil from the roots and replace it with potting mixture.

Even the experienced grower sometimes finds it difficult to predict how well a pot will drain. A fairly deep pot with a flat bottom and perpendicular sides does not usually drain well, but there are exceptions. Occasionally a deep bowl, which would appear to promise perfect drainage, turns out to be disappointing. The tree should be lifted from the container and enough of its bottom roots removed to make room for one or two inches of gravel. Soil left in a coarse seive after the finer particles have dropped through can also be used. Providing additional drainage holes or enlarging the present ones will also solve the problem.

Water may not flow through the soil if it was packed too firmly when the tree was potted, either because the grower was too zealous or because the soil was too damp. Most of the old soil should be removed and replaced.

Some species have such a mass of fine roots that once they have nearly filled the pot they retard drainage. If the drainage was good for a few months after the tree was potted but has become progressively worse, this is a probable cause. Removing about one-third of the roots will eliminate the trouble.

A possible cause of poor drainage, but one that can easily be avoided, is the wrong potting mixture. If the soil in a rather large pot has been sifted through a too fine mesh, or if fine beach sand has been used instead of sharp river sand, the mixture may pack and retard drainage. The solution is to replace the soil with a coarser mixture.

From here on, growing potted trees is simply a repetition of the steps described in these first eight chapters. There is nothing else the reader must do to have small, healthy plants that he may shape and train any way he wishes as he faces the pleasant, leisurely task of turning his potted trees into finished bonsai.

Chapter IX

SHORT CUTS

In the world of the purely aesthetic Japanese grower, to whom tradition is as much a part of bonsai as are branches, roots, and leaves, *money* is a word to be avoided. Americans are all too likely to ask, "How old is it?" and "How much is it worth?" on viewing a beautiful dwarfed tree for the first time. The Japanese do not put a monetary value on their best old trees because none are for sale.

In both Japan and the United States, however, there are commercial growers of dwarfed trees, and the saying "Time is money" might well have been originated by them. The more years a grower spends readying a tree for market, the more he must charge for it. The higher the price, the fewer the customers. Saving time and labor to keep prices within reason is therefore just as essential whether the products to be sold are bonsai, automobiles, or ready-to-wear.

The home grower does not usually develop his trees for profit, but if he is eager to see them increase in size and value as quickly as possible, he would be wise to study the methods of those who do. He can then follow or modify these methods to suit his own purposes.

Since any plant will develop more slowly in a pot than in the open ground, many commercial growers allow their young trees to remain in the field for from three to ten years. Trees suitable for developing by this method are those started from seed, nursery plants in one-gallon or smaller containers, slow-growing trees, and small specimens of hard-to-find species that have been purchased by mail.

Uncontrolled growth will quickly change the form of the tree, so this method is recommended only for young trees whose shapes have not yet been determined. A partly trained tree should be grown in a pot.

The tree kept in open ground must, of course, be winter-hardy in the grower's area. How long he allows it to remain there depends on his patience; the longer he can wait, the larger and more attractive the trunk will become.

Any sunny spot in the yard where the soil is well-drained and of about the same quality as that supporting the usual garden plant is suitable for the purpose. In early spring, before the buds have opened, the young trees are planted from twelve to eighteen inches apart or far enough to prevent their roots and tops from interfering with each other. There are now three methods of handling the tree:

The first and most timesaving method avoids any action whatever that will slow a tree's growth. Since nature tends to maintain a balance, when the top is trimmed back during a growing period root growth slows down or stops altogether for a while. When the tree is dormant, however, roots are less affected by the trimming of branches. The branches are therefore cut back severely when the tree is first planted. As a result, the first growth of spring finds the supply from the roots much greater than the demand from the top. Strong new branches will then be put out in an attemtp to regain the tree's normal balance, and in this way the trunk will increase in size at the fastest possible rate.

If this principle is understood, it becomes evident that the tree should never be pruned while it is still growing. A minimum amount of thinning and shortening of branches may be done at the end of the first growing period, which occurs about midsummer for most species. At that time also, any suckers that may have appeared should be removed.

The following spring and each spring thereafter, before buds have opened, the tree is again cut back severely and midsummer pruning is held to a minimum.

The year before the tree is dug and potted, its roots are treated like those of a natural tree being dug for the first time. That is, a circular cut is made around the tree about ten or twelve inches from the trunk and ten inches deep, leaving a few of the side roots intact. The following spring these roots are cut, and the tree is lifted from the ground and potted.

As when transplanting any tree, as much soil should be retained around the roots as possible. The roots of a deciduous tree may then be cut back severely, those of a conifer somewhat less.

The disadvantage of this method compared with the two that follow is that the shape of the tree cannot be controlled as it grows. Since so little pruning is done, if a dense head of small twigs is desired it must be developed in the years after the tree is potted.

In the second method the roots are left untouched, just as they were in the first. Branch ends, however, are pinched back constantly, whenever unwanted growth appears, without regard to the growing periods of the tree. This slows its growth rate and the trunk does not develop as quickly as in the first method, but when the tree is potted it will already have a good shape and will require less training. The roots are cut underground the year before the tree is potted, in the manner previously described.

The third method is the slowest of all, though the trunk will still increase in size at a much faster rate than that of a pot-grown tree. Each spring, for as long as it is left in the ground, the tree is lifted and its long side roots and tap root are cut back to within five or six inches of the trunk. Most of the fibrous roots are left untouched. The top is kept under control, as in the second method. Constant pinching back of the tips encourages branching, and the tree maintains a good shape throughout the years it is kept in the ground. It may be lifted any spring the grower wishes to pot it, and its roots can be trimmed back immediately to fit the container.

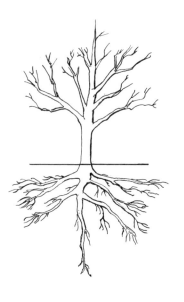

Roots not touched, top cut
back in early spring.

Roots not touched, top cut
back all summer.

Roots trimmed once a year,
top cut back all summer.

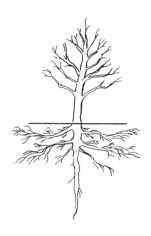

This last method is the one preferred by the writer for most species. Roots are always kept under control, so that a tree can be lifted
the eighth or tenth year as easily and safely as it can the third or
fourth, and without year-ahead planning. In addition, though de-

velopment is comparatively slow, it is fast enough to make open-ground growing well worth while, as shown by these two four-year-old Siberian elms. Both were started from seed at the same time. One was pot-grown from the beginning, while the other was planted in the ground when it was about six months old and cared for as in this third method. The difference in trunk sizes and density of the crowns, already obvious, will become even greater as time goes on.

Siberian elm grown in open ground for four years has far outdistanced, in trunk size and density of twig growth, a pot-grown elm of the same species and age.

In general, either the first or second method is preferable for trees that grow slowly. Deciduous trees that send out long branches in a few weeks' time are better kept under control by the second or third method. Pines, oaks, sweetgums, and nut trees, all rather difficult to transplant, are more easily lifted for potting when the third method is used. It is up to the grower to decide which method will best fit his purposes and the growth habits of a particular species.

Compared with pot-grown trees, those growing in open ground require little care. Since they need to be watered no more often than other garden plants, it is almost as easy to grow ten or twenty as one or two. A dozen or more seedling trees of the same species, intended for a bonsai forest planting, can easily be brought to potting size by leaving them in the ground for a few years. Small, young trees found growing naturally, which may or may not be usable later, can be left in the ground to see how they develop. Open ground is a convenient place to grow expendable trees for experimental purposes.

In short, the grower would be wise to use a lavish hand when planting small trees in his garden. He can always discard the surplus (if he has the courage), but in four or five years he may well regret the time lost if he has started with too few.

The free-fruiting quality of fig trees grown in pots off-sets the disadvantage of rather large leaves.

The same tree two years earlier, before training was begun.

In spite of its rather large leaves, the ginkgo has long been a popular subject for bonsai.

PART II

The Art of Growing Bonsai

Chapter X

PRUNING AND SHAPING

S INCE MANY growers consider the transformation of potted trees into bonsai the most interesting part of the work, it is too much to ask of the novice that he wait at least one full year before starting to shape his trees. Discussion of this art, however, has been delayed until now in order to give it its proper place. A young tree can be shaped too soon. Within reason, it cannot be shaped too late.

Just as the connoisseur can name the artist of an unsigned painting by its style and brushwork, it is said that in Japan an expert grower can study a fine bonsai and know which of his colleagues has trained it. This "signature" is more inevitable than desirable, however, for though a painting should reflect the artist's style, a tree should reflect its own. The grower's skill is in emphasizing or improving a tree's best lines and characteristics, not in manufacturing them.

This is more easily said than done. To some the straight-trunked, upright shape is the most appealing, because it duplicates many of the trees seen in the countryside. To others the twisted, slanting shape is preferable, because it suggests the Orient and familiar pictures of classical, ancient bonsai. Still others are drawn immediately to bonsai with wind-swept or cascade shapes, or to multiple plantings.

Most of the time a grower is unaware of his partiality to one style. Nevertheless if he were to start with small seedlings that as yet had no time to develop characteristics of their own and shape each according to his own taste, there would almost inevitably be an uninteresting similarity in them by the time they had reached a good size.

But not all newly acquired trees are shaped in this way. Those bought in a nursery were probably selected because of some unusual line of trunk or branches. Naturally dwarfed trees have, of course, formed their own basic shapes many years ago. Training such trees along their already acquired lines may be started as soon as they are potted. However, in the early collection of any grower, there will certainly be a number of young trees with thin, straight trunks and sparse branches. The longer he can wait for each to develop its own "personality," the more successful the finished bonsai will be.

This Sargent juniper, found in a nursery, was grown in the open ground for a year before it was potted and shaped.

Many authors suggest training the small tree to duplicate the shape the particular species takes when growing naturally. In many cases this is good advice, but there are two reasons it should not be accepted as a fixed rule. A dozen trees of the same species, each growing in a different area, may have twelve different shapes. Also, unless a grower limits his collection to species with which he is thoroughly familiar, he will have no idea how some of his trees should look. Finding out would involve elaborate research. But if he gives them enough time without forcing his own ideas on them with wire and pruning shears, most of them will show him.

Swiss stone pine, with the naturally curved trunk characteristic of all stone pines.

It is sometimes also advised that the height of a tree be shortened by bending the trunk into an S-shaped curve. Such practice should be viewed with skepticism. Dwarfed trees grown for commercial purposes are sometimes handled this way, but one never sees such artificial shaping in the beautiful old trees of Japan. A tree with a tall, thin trunk that does not branch reasonably low is not suitable bonsai material, and no amount of shaping will conceal this fact.

This is not to say that a tree should never be trained into unusual lines, but that these lines should not look unnatural or devised. Should a tree's developing shape suggest a cascade style, for example, there is no regulation that prevents the grower from bending it down and planting it in a tall pot. It may turn out to be one of his best bonsai. Again, good taste and a trained eye should guide him. With these, common sense, and a knowledge of tree habits, the grower can make his own rules as he goes along.

Studying the trees themselves will tell him more clearly than words just how they should be shaped. Although each has its own characteristics and should therefore be different from any other when training and shaping has been completed, here are six points they should have in common to merit the name of bonsai:

> An appearance of age
> A relatively thick trunk
> No visible evidence of pruning
> No scars from careless training
> Many twigs or dense needle clumps
> An unobscured trunk line

AGE

Although a bonsai does not have to be old to be successful, it should be made to look as old as possible. It is not difficult to add many years to the appearance of a potted tree by artificial means. A young, natural tree is thick and bushy, its branches grow upward, and its trunk is smooth and thin. Removing some branches of the small tree and encouraging the lower ones to curve downwards with wires, ties, or weights will eliminate these two signs of immaturity.

Only time or unusual growing conditions will thicken and gnarl a trunk, a good reason why the grower should pay special attention to this portion when selecting a tree for dwarfing.

A RELATIVELY THICK TRUNK

Since all size is relative, a trunk will look thin only if the tree is too tall or the pot selected for it too large. The trunk may therefore be thickened in minutes by shortening the tree and moving it to a smaller container. If a smaller tree is not wanted, the only alternative is to increase trunk size by giving the tree ample growing room for a few more years.

EVIDENCE OF PRUNING

There should be no stubs or obvious signs of shortened branches or trunks. This will be covered in detail when pruning is discussed.

SCARS FROM CARELESS TRAINING

It seems almost too obvious to mention that care should be taken when handling a potted tree not to scrape or gouge its bark, yet this is often done by careless growers. Most of these injuries will disappear in time, but until they have healed they will detract from the tree's appearance.

Wires that have been left on too long will leave ridges in the bark that may never disappear entirely. The usual advice that a wire should be removed from a branch at the end of a year is too general. The wood of some trees, such as the weeping fig and the stone pines, is quite soft and can be marred by wires in just a few months. In addition, the growth rate of the tree and the amount of pressure exerted by the wire are important in determining how long it may remain. An examination should be made of the wires every few months to see which are beginning to press into the bark. Some wires may be left in place for two years or more, if necessary, while others must be removed in from three to six months. In the latter case, if the branch has not yet become fixed in its new position, it may be rewired. Care should be taken, however, that the wire does not touch the bark in the same places as before.

Twigs and needle clumps

One very often sees a small tree that fulfills most of the requirements of a successful bonsai. Its shape is good, container size is appropriate, branches are well spaced, and trunk line is excellent. Yet it has no *gei*. Even the untrained viewer, not conscious of why it has not caught and held his attention, will pass it by.

It has failed because of the condition of its branches. A young tree straight from the nursery may have many branches, but most of them will be long with few side branches of their own. A potted tree with too few secondary branches and twigs cannot accurately be called a bonsai. When properly pruned and trained, a deciduous tree may have relatively few main branches, but these will end in dense clumps of small twigs. In conifers this same multiple branching will result in solid, tight clumps of needles.

It is virtually impossible to find a young tree in a nursery or growing naturally that is already branched in this way. Only constant shortening or pinching of new growth and root trimming when the tree is repotted will bring it about. Proper treatment of branch ends will begin to show results during the first season, and leaf clumps will become tighter and more attractive each year.

With a few exceptions that will be mentioned later, the tips of deciduous trees are pinched back all during the growing season. Two pairs of leaves are usually left on the lower branches, one pair on the upper. This will widen the crown at the base. If a tall, columnar shape is desired, a single pair of leaves may be left on both the lower and upper branches. Again, this is not a rule. The grower may shape the tree as he wishes, allowing as many leaf buds to remain on each branch as he thinks advisable. No single new shoot, however, should be allowed to grow too long before it is encouraged to branch. When the tree is older, long, undivided branches will spoil its appearance.

Conifers such as junipers, arborvitae, and cypresses, are handled in this same way; part of the new growth is removed as it appears. Single shoots that grow from buds at the tips of branches on such trees as spruce, fir, and cedar are pinched back to within half an inch or so of the old growth.

Pines usually put out their whole year's growth in the spring and are treated a little differently. When each pale green, candlelike shoot is partly open, it is held firmly at the base and the portion to be removed is twisted off gently. On mature pines only a few needles of the new growth are allowed to remain, but one-third to one-half of the new shoot is left on younger trees to make them increase in size faster. Care should be taken always to leave part of the new growth. Its complete removal from most species will halt the growth of the branch permanently.

Some fruiting and flowering trees are cared for differently. The pomegranate, butterfly bush, and crape myrtle, for example, carry their flower buds on the tips of new shoots. If these are removed, there will be no blooms; so the grower must choose between the constant shaping of his tree and the pleasure of flowers. The long shoots may be cut back after their blooming period. But as this does not occur with some species until midsummer or later, the strong growth of spring and early summer must grow untouched. Mature trees in this group are usually allowed to bloom before branches are trimmed. With young trees, however, it is generally wiser to forego flowers for a few years in order to encourage branching, with the promise of a more profuse bloom and a better shaped tree later on.

This Norway spruce shows the effects of continual pinching back of branch tips. Clumps will become tight and dense as care continues.

The start of future bonsai. From left to right: A Savin juniper in its nursery container. Transplanted to a bonsai container. The trunk is revealed

On year-old branches of some fruit trees such as apricot, peach, apple, and cherry, flower buds form in the fall for bloom the following spring. Branches should therefore be cut back only after the blooming period. In most localities new shoots may be controlled until about the first of August, when the dry spell begins, and should not be touched again until the tree has bloomed the following spring.

On still another class of trees the flower buds and fruit do not form on the tips of the branches but farther down, from the third to the seventh leaf eyes. Holly, fig, persimmon, chestnut, and citrus trees are examples. If desired, their tips may be pinched back as they grow, but heavy pruning should be delayed until the dormant season.

As a rule if a bonsai has only a few distinctive separate clumps of leaf growth, three, five, or seven of them are more pleasing to the eye than an even number of two, four, or six. If there are more points of interest than this, the eye does not distinguish as readily between them. Whether they are of an odd or even number becomes less important.

Lower branches appear. Final shaping to clean-cut lines. In future years tree will become dwarfed, branch clumps will thicken.

AN UNOBSCURED TRUNK LINE

Since the trunk is usually the most important feature of a bonsai, everything possible should be done to emphasize and reveal its lines. Some shade trees, especially elms and zelkovas, are often trained to grow a thick, solid crown of leaves, and the trunks are revealed only from their bases to the lower branches. The leaves of most other trees, however, are usually trained to grow in clumps. The branches are pruned so that the eye automatically follows the line of the trunk by catching generous glimpses of it from base to tip. This again is a method of adding years to a tree's appearance, for the trunks of mature natural trees are usually visible in this way.

Pruning

The best time for heavy pruning is the same as that for potting, in the four or five weeks of early spring, before leaf buds open. A potted tree usually receives such pruning only once, when shaping is first begun. After that only small branches need be removed occasionally, and most trees will not complain if this is done during any season.

Nearly all trees, whether full-sized or dwarfed, have one side that is more attractive than the other. The grower should study his potted tree carefully and decide from which angle it will be viewed when completed. Pruning and wiring will then be done with this in mind.

Needless to say, each branch should be studied carefully before it is cut off. Unless the grower has years of experience behind him, the pruning of a good-sized tree, thick with growth, should not be completed in one session. A doubtful branch may look entirely different tomorrow, next week, or even next year, than it does today. It may suggest a new and better way of shaping the tree than was originally planned.

Branches that are obviously undesirable should be removed first. This includes one of two that cross each other, one of two that are parallel and growing close together, and thin, clustered branches on the trunk close to heavy ones. Scrubby dead wood may be removed, but thick dead branches should be kept until it is certain they are not wanted; the *gei* of a finished tree can depend solely on such a branch, either stripped of bark and bleached, or left as it is. Extremely long branches may be shortened.

Preliminary pruning completed, the grower should stop trimming for a while. The tree may be left for another day or carried into the house and studied from time to time. If the pruning is unhurried, one by one undesirable branches will almost beg to be taken off. One step will lead to another. The first pruning of a new tree is a slow process, but too absorbing ever to be called tedious.

Cuts should be made with sharp tools. Special bonsai tools are excellent, but scissors or ordinary nail clippers will do very well for small branches and garden shears, if designed to permit close work, for larger ones. A fine-toothed saw is sometimes necessary for very thick wood.

If a branch is to be shortened, the cut should be slanted and should face the back of the tree if possible. Always cut just above a bud or leaf cluster so that no unsightly stub is left. A thick branch should be shortened at the point where another branch joins it. If an entire branch is removed, it should be cut flush with the trunk.

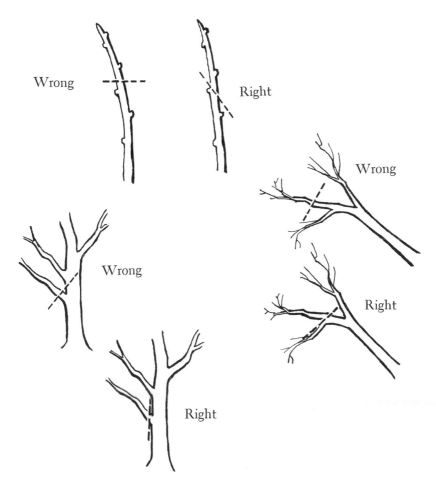

Though not necessary, it is good practice to cover all but very small cuts with pitch. This not only prevents disease from entering the wounds, but improves the appearance of the tree until fresh bark has had time to cover them.

Wires and ties

For many years the Japanese have changed the shapes of their bonsai by annealing copper wire in the embers of a rice-straw fire and then coiling the wire around a branch. The branch is then bent to the desired shape, and when it has become set in that position the wire is removed.

This does the job, but so will simpler methods. Many branches need no wiring at all, but if one does, any rustproof wire such as aluminum, galvanized iron, or copper (not necessarily annealed) is satisfactory.

The grower can use any method to hold a branch in a desired position, as long as it does not injure the tree. Branches growing too close together may be separated by a round stone or short stick. If they are too far apart, a short tie will bring them closer. Two oppo-

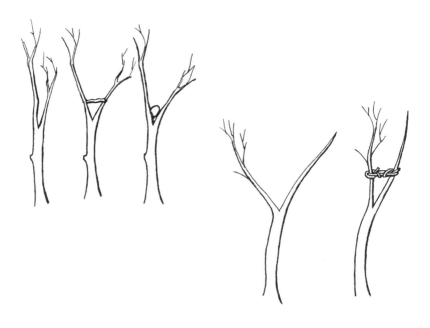

site bottom branches may be lowered by bringing a length of cord
or wire under the pot and fastening an end to each branch. A single
branch may be lowered in much the same way. The cord is brought
under the pot, one end is fastened to the branch, and the other is
tied to the base of the trunk. If lower branches are thick and sturdy
or if they have been tied, upper branches may then be pulled down
by means of ties fastened to branches below them.

Instead of wiring, small weights may be used to make branches weep. These are fastened near their tips. Or a handful of half-inch metal bolt washers from the hardware store may be threaded on a wire, which is then fastened around the training pot just below the rim. One end of a length of string is then tied to a branch, the other slipped through a washer and knotted. This is a more convenient method than the much-used one of lacing the pot with a network of cord, to which the string ends are then attached.

Straightening a trunk by tying it to a stake is the traditional method. If the trunk is not too thick it may be straightened by means of a single length of wire or stout cord tied as shown in the drawing below. Conversely, a straight trunk may be curved the same way.

If a tied trunk is so thick it cannot be straightened all at once, a double wire or cord may be fastened to the tree. An ordinary wooden plant label is slipped between the two lines at the edge of the pot. The tension on the trunk can then be increased gradually by giving the label a few turns every week or so.

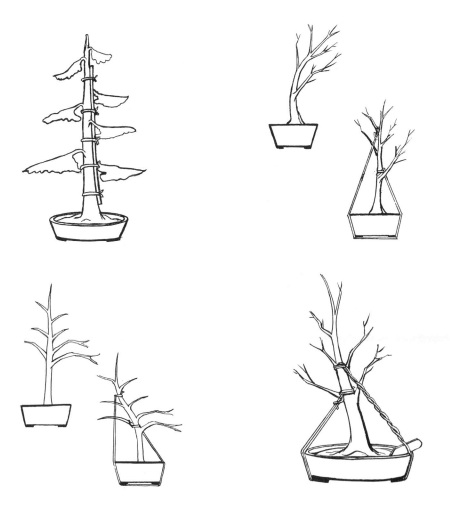

A trunk or heavy branch may be curved by means of a metal rod or a narrow, flat bar that is first bent to the desired shape. The trunk or branch is then tied to the metal with strong cord. In most cases, when this method is used, the bark should first be protected by wrapping it with strips of cloth or heavy paper.

If wire is used as a tie and pressure on the branch will be heavy or prolonged, the danger of cutting the wood can be eliminated by wrapping the branch with several thicknesses of cloth or paper at the point where the wire is to be attached.

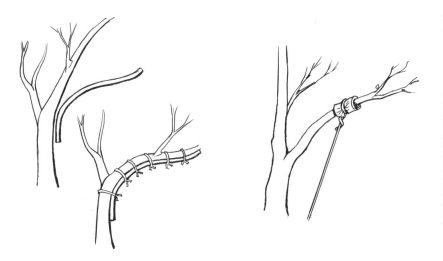

If the top of a tree is to be cut back and a short side branch trained as a leader, much work can be saved if the unwanted wood is cut only part way back and the remaining stub used as a stake to which the side branch is tied. When the leader has become permanently set in its new position, the stub is cut off on a slant at the base.

Although any strong cord may be used for tying, the green, plastic-covered wire found in almost any garden shop or nursery is most convenient. A twist of the ends fastens it in position, the plastic cover helps prevent it from cutting into the branch, and it will not rot and break as quickly as cord even though it may be kept constantly damp.

The methods given, plus any the grower may devise, will take care of many shaping problems. There will still, however, be branches in such positions that wire must be used. If the trunk is to be shaped with wire, one end is pushed into the soil at the base of the tree and the rest coiled to the top. It is then bent into the desired position.

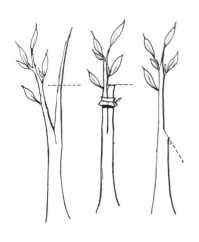

In shaping a side branch, the wire is fastened to the trunk and coiled to the tip of the branch. For an outer branch the wire is fastened a little below the point where it joins another branch.

The wire should always be tight enough to hold the branch in position, but never so tight that it cuts into the bark. Shaping a wired branch does not have to be done all at once. If the wood is stiff or brittle, it should be bent a little more each week or so, to prevent the danger of its snapping under too much sudden pressure.

Chapter XI

POTS, STONES, AND GROUND COVERS

Selecting a suitable pot for a particular bonsai is comparable to finding the right frame for a painting. The two should be in such harmony that the viewer is unaware the whole that so pleases him is actually made of two units, each of which would lose a great deal without the other. Though selecting a good pot is of the utmost importance, it does not follow that it must be of a particular shape or color, for most bonsai will look well in any of several different containers.

Special bonsai pots come in various depths, widths, shapes, colors, and glazes, but they should all have one thing in common: simplicity. Colors are usually muted; designs, if any, are either etched into the pot or raised in relief, but are not prominent enough to attract special attention. They may be square, round, hexagonal, oval, rectangular, or diamond-shaped; but novel, irregular shapes or those with fluted or scalloped edges should be avoided. They tend to distract attention from the simplicity and beauty of the tree.

Wood, as mentioned earlier, is one of the best materials for containers, from the standpoint of the health of the tree. This should encourage the grower who wishes to make his own, for homemade containers can be just as attractive as those made commercially, often more so. Any rot-resistant wood, such as redwood or pecky cypress, may be used. Again, simplicity is the keynote. The writer's

137

opinion, contrary to that of some growers, is that such pots should be carefully made and well finished. The casual, roughhewn look does not seem to blend well with the near-perfect beauty of properly grown bonsai.

As a rule-of-thumb, symmetrical trees are usually planted in round, square, or hexagonal pots; cascade or drooping styles in fairly deep ones; and trees with slanting or sweeping lines in oval or rectangular pots. If the pot is round or has sides of equal length, the tree is planted in the center, if rectangular or oval, about one-third of the distance from one end.

Tradition has it that trees of certain species and ages should be grown in pots of specified colors and glazes, but again it is better that good taste and personal preference guide the American grower. Common sense will tell him, for example, that an orange-flowering quince should not be planted in a red pot and one that produces white flowers would be beautiful in the white container traditionally used for conifers.

Whatever the shape or color, the pot selected should be of a size to hold the least amount of soil that will support the life of the tree. A very narrow pot would not suit a broad, spreading tree, but the wider pot selected should be fairly shallow, so that no more soil is used than necessary. In general, the height of an erect tree should be at least three or four times the depth of its container, and the whole composition is usually more pleasing to the eye if the branches extend beyond the width of the pot.

Ground covers

In many countries, including Japan, moss is a symbol of age. Because of this, and because it is easy to find and grow, it has always been a favorite ground cover for bonsai. A fine, green layer on the soil serves four purposes:

It heightens the illusion of age.
By resembling grass in miniature, it adds to the feeling that the bonsai is a faithful copy of a full-sized tree.
It holds moisture in the soil.
If the soil has an uneven surface, it prevents sloping areas from being washed flat by rain.

In the moist, shaded areas of almost any lawn, small, velvety patches of moss can be found. It grows between the cracks of brick walks and patios or on the north side of a large tree, shaded by the wide trunk. Small pieces can be lifted and pressed into the soil of the pot, where they will soon spread to cover the entire surface. Any that is not used can be dried, powdered, and stored in jars for future use. The powder is sprinkled lightly over the soil of a newly potted tree and watered carefully until it begins to grow again.

In spring or fall, an hour or so spent in the woods will yield many more species of moss than can be found around the average garden. Many wood mosses will not return to life after having been dried and powdered, however, so patches should be pressed into the soil of a seed flat and kept moist and shaded until they are needed.

All species of moss need some shade in which to flourish. Moss cannot be grown on the soil of a bonsai that is kept in full sun, unless its branches are wide and spreading enough to furnish protection. Many other ground covers, however, do well in varying amounts of light. Baby's tears, readily obtainable in areas of the country where winters are not too severe, is a much used cover.

Dwarf creeping thyme, with its minute white flowers, does very well in sunlight that is too bright for moss. Any tiny, green plant with spreading habits and shallow roots is suitable. Since there are many to choose from, each grower can probably discover several as yet unused for this purpose that will be successful for him.

Stones

An occasional, beautiful stone, preferably with moss growing on it, can very suitably by placed with some species of trees such as stone or mountain pines or coastal cypresses. A tabulation, however, of the trees in four books showing the finest old Japanese bonsai resulted in these figures: 123 trees, 1 with a stone; 89 trees, 4 with a stone; 84 trees, 1 with a stone; 17 trees, no stones—a total of 6 stones on the soil of 313 trees. None of the bonsai had the handfuls of small stones seen so often on the soil of the untrained, newly potted trees of inexperienced American growers.

It is unlikely that a viewer would ever say of a beautiful and skill-fully trained tree, "I wonder why there are no stones," although he might very well remark, "All that clutter spoils the effect."

This is purely the opinion of the writer, however, and should be considered as such by those who have a particular fondness for stones. As in almost every other phase of growing bonsai, personal preference and good taste should be the final authority.

Miscellaneous decorating materials

Creating miniature scenes by adding small figures, houses, bridges, and the like, is a separate art in Japan, called *bonkei*. The grower might enjoy trying his hand at making one or two of these delight-ful, small arrangements.

With bonsai, however, the tree is all-important. Nothing should be added that will draw attention from it. In the writer's opinion driftwood and other extraneous materials tend to produce a cluttered effect, just as stones do. Too little is better than too much, and none at all is seldom a mistake.

Lava rock, light and easily hollowed with chisel and hammer, makes an attractive container for this seven-year-old Mugho pine.

Chapter XII

SPECIAL PLANTING STYLES

A SINGLE tree in a container in which the soil is level or slightly mounded is the classical style for bonsai. Most dwarfed trees are planted in this way.

However, as the grower becomes more adept and the problem of keeping his trees alive and well no longer absorbs his attention, he is very apt to long for an occasional new world to conquer. Here are a few, none of them really difficult, that sooner or later he may want to try:

> Forests and group plantings
> Forests from single trees
> Trees planted on stones
> Multiple-trunk bonsai
> Bonsai from tree stumps
> Exposed roots

FORESTS AND GROUP PLANTINGS

There is something about a miniature forest that appeals to everyone, and even small collections usually include at least one. Unlike the newly potted young tree alone in its container, a group of such trees together gives the impression of a mature, fairyland forest from the moment it is planted. And it will become more effective and convincing with each year that passes.

If forests and group plantings are to last indefinitely, all trees should be of the same species. Though plants of all kinds can grow side by side in the open ground, confined in a pot one species will sooner or later win the race for the available nourishment and growing room. The others will weaken and eventually die. Group plantings of mixed species can live for some years, however. If longevity is not particularly desired, two or more species may be combined, provided of course they look well together. In most cases the one-species planting is more attractive.

Any small-leaved deciduous trees such as maples, elms, or zelkovas are suitable. Among the conifers, cryptomerias, larches, and short-needled spruces, such as the Yedo spruce, are often used. Since pines die easily when grown in groups, the inexperienced grower would do well to avoid them in multiple plantings.

Bonsai forests appeal to everyone. These trident maples have been in their container for less than two years.

Forests should be planted in shallow oval or rectangular trays. If the trees are seedlings, a year or two in the open ground or in separate pots will give them a chance to increase in size before they are planted together. Once confined they must compete with each other, and their growth rate will slow down considerably.

Since the roots of deciduous trees may be cut back severely in spring, it is easy to fit them into a shallow container. If conifer roots are long and thick, however, an intermediate step of root trimming serves as added insurance against loss. The tap root and long side roots should be cut back one season; the following spring they may then be trimmed short enough to fit into the container. As in single plantings, the roots may be wired; but because it will be necessary to remove the wires in a year or so, it is better to cut or spread the roots wherever possible.

It is often impossible to fit roots into a very shallow tray so that the soil level will be flat. This should present no problem since a gradual mounding of earth from the edges to the center of the tray can be very effective.

In forest plantings trees are usually graduated in height, with the tallest near the center or at one end. They may be erect, or slanted as if wind-blown, and should not be evenly spaced but grouped casually as they might be in a full-sized forest. It is also more pleasing if an open area of two or three inches is left all around between the edge of the planting and the edge of the pot.

Group plantings differ from forests in that there are fewer trees, and they are usually placed quite close together to give the effect of a single tree with several trunks. As with forests, trees in group plantings will develop more slowly than trees grown alone, so it is better to start with plants that already have fair-sized trunks. This is more important in a group than a forest planting, because the trunks of a few trees are more noticeable than those of many clustered together.

Even if the trees in a forest are all the same species, there will still be competition between them for growing room. Occasionally one or two will suddenly take hold and start to grow more quickly than the others. Once started, the process is apt to snowball. The growth rate of the stronger trees may continue to increase, while that of the others may slow down to the point where their lives are threatened. If this should happen, the roots of the more robust trees should be trimmed severely during the next repotting. In this way the weaker trees will again have an equal chance in the race for survival.

Center tree in this four-year-old Japanese black pine forest is winning the race for growing room. If not controlled, it may eventually endanger the lives of the others.

The stones retained moisture in the soil for first three years.

FORESTS FROM SINGLE TREES

A single tree, usually a conifer, may be planted in such a way that the branches become the trees of the forest. Since there is only one root system, competition is eliminated and the tree will grow at a normal rate of speed. Because of lack of competition, pine forests can be developed successfully in this way.

When a single tree is used, however, the grower cannot expect his planting to resemble a full-sized forest for at least four or five years; the individual branches must be given time to develop many branches of their own before they will look like trees.

Before planting, branches on one side are wired and bent so that they will protrude, erect and approximately parallel, from the surface of the soil. The remaining branches are cut off. The tree is then planted horizontally in a shallow container at a depth that barely covers the trunk and base of each branch.

Since the lower trunk and root system must occupy one end of the container, the tree selected should branch very low so that the individual "trees" can be well spaced from one end of the tray to the other. If they are still pushed too far off center by a large root system, it may gradually be reduced in subsequent repottings and the whole forest shifted to the center of the tray.

TREES PLANTED ON STONES

Planting a tree in such a way that the upper portion of its roots are exposed and clinging to the surface of a large stone looks difficult to do, but is really quite simple. When the tree is young and its roots still supple, it is fastened with wires or ties to the top of the stone. The roots are brought down the sides and their tips buried in the soil of a shallow container. The rock is then plastered with a thick paste of peat moss and water and the whole covered with sphagnum moss, which is tied in place. About a year later, after the roots have become established in the pot, the mosses are gradually removed until the bare rock with the roots clinging to it is fully exposed.

About one-third of the sphagnum moss is removed at first, starting at the top. The peat moss thus exposed will be washed away
during normal waterings of the tree. This procedure is repeated
until the whole rock is exposed and washed clean.

Training a tree to grow on
a stone. Left, a Mugho
pine, its roots spread on a
stone and covered with
moss. Below, the following
year. Moss partly removed
after root tips have become
established in soil in container.

Left, about ten months
later, roots now fully exposed.

As the tree matures, the planting will be more attractive if only a few thick roots cling to the rock. For this reason many recommend that all but three or four of the main roots be cut off at the base of the trunk before the tree is planted. Since this only weakens the tree, however, it is safer to leave all the roots intact until the tree is growing well on the rock. The small, unwanted roots may then be snipped away, a few at a time, until only a few of the heavier ones are left.

It has been pointed out that roots always grow towards water. If the roots of the tree are not long enough to reach the soil in the container, they may be lengthened by a simple method based on this principle. The tree is planted in a deep pot and watered only from the bottom. If the top half of the soil is kept rather dry, the roots will reach the bottom of the pot in a short time. The tree can then be moved to the rock.

MULTIPLE-TRUNK BONSAI

A dwarfed tree with several trunks has much the same appeal as a forest, but has the advantage of a single root system. It therefore grows at a normal rate and is easy to care for and to repot.

There are so many trees of this style to choose from, both in nurseries and growing naturally, that much time will be saved if one is found that is already of a good size. If the grower wishes to make his own, however, he can do so by planting a deciduous tree in open ground and cutting off the above-ground growth. Its supply-and-demand system thus thrown off balance, in most cases the tree will quickly send up suckers. As many of these as desired may be removed as soon as they appear and the rest trained to grow as separate trunks. The tree should be left in the ground until these new trunks have thickened and become somewhat woody. It may then be dug, in the proper season, and potted.

There is a Japanese superstition that the even numbers, with the exception of two, are unlucky. As a result, Japanese growers look with disfavor on trees with four, six, or eight trunks. Here again, whether the grower chooses to grow a tree with three or four trunks depends on his taste and how much he respects tradition. Like the points of interest in leaf clumps, it seems to the writer that a tree with three trunks can usually be trained into a more artistic shape than can one with four, but that as the number increases, the issue decreases in importance. It becomes negligible when a difference of eight versus nine trunks, for example, is involved.

An American red maple growing in the multiple-trunk style.

Bonsai from tree stumps

A gnarled, old stump with leafy branches growing from it is always a much prized possession of the grower lucky enough to find an attractive one. Old, neglected orchards, the edges of cleared fields, vacant property in the city where trees have been cut down in past years, are all promising areas to search.

If the grower cannot find just the stump he is looking for, he can make his own. A deciduous tree whose trunk is heavy and gnarled at the base, may be cut to within five or six inches of the ground. Since the trunk will still be alive, suckers may grow from it, or they may appear at ground level. Either way, the stump will be promising bonsai material.

All that is needed to start it on its way to becoming a valuable, potted plant is a little knowledge—and muscle. The root system is handled in the same way as that of a naturally dwarfed tree. The roots are cut back, and the stump is given time to develop new fibrous roots at its base. It is then lifted in early spring and planted in the ground under cutting-bed conditions. If summer growth indicates the root system is in good condition, the stump may be potted in early fall or, preferably, the following spring. This intermediate step of a season or a year in the open ground may be omitted, and the stump potted as soon as it is lifted, but in this way its chances for survival are lessened.

If the stump is too wide to be attractive or to fit into the container, any portion of it may be split off as long as a sufficient number of fibrous roots remain attached to it.

In some trees the trunk and branches have died, but the roots are still alive. Suckers, if any, will then appear at ground level. When potted, the live branches will be at the base of such a stump. This may or may not be attractive, depending on its shape and the grower's ingenuity. The finished planting is apt to have more *gei* if the trunk is cut off at ground level. The upper portion of the roots, with suckers attached, is then planted above the soil level in the pot.

In this way the root section becomes a substitute for the above-ground stump.

The wistaria on the opposite page was handled in this manner. A large section of the root was dug, planted in the garden, and left alone for a year. At the end of this time, roots from the suckers were five or six inches long. It was then potted, and the entire plant was covered with the same peat-moss-and-water paste and sphagnum-moss blanket used in the roots-on-rock planting. After the suckers had developed into branches and their roots were well established, the large, dead root was exposed and washed clean.

EXPOSED ROOTS

A bonsai that fans out at soil level has far more *gei* than one without gradation in width, which enters the ground like a post. A few heavy roots exposed at the base of the trunk also help add to the illusion of age.

Exposing roots and trunk base is a simple thing to do. During repotting, the tree is set a little higher in the container than before. Since underground roots will increase in size more quickly than those exposed to the air, a mound of soil covered with moss may be kept over the lifted roots until they have become as thick as desired. The moss is then removed and the soil washed flat during normal waterings. Fine hair roots thus exposed, which will detract from the importance of the larger ones, may be cut away a few at a time.

An irregularly shaped bonsai may have exposed roots that extend from only one side of the tree, but roots of a symmetrical tree should be symmetrical, too, radiating from the trunklike wheel spokes. This, however, is the ideal. It may safely be said that any thick roots showing at the base of the trunk will add to the appearance of any dwarfed tree.

Base of this interesting bonsai is a dead root section of an old wistaria tree.

Pieris japonica, with its naturally rough bark and irregular shape, is a good species for bonsai.

Chapter XIII

FROM THE WRITER'S NOTEBOOK

To the grower in search of promising material, knowing the species of a small, well-shaped tree found growing naturally is important only if it can help him in his future handling of it. If it is a hardy maple, whether it is A. *rubrum* or A. *saccharum* makes little practical difference. He knows by now that if he digs it in early spring there is a very good chance it will survive the transplanting. Similarly he knows that a pine, whatever its species, will require more careful handling. He does not need to be told if its needles are long or short. He can see for himself. The fact that a tree will bear fruit or flowers or berries is of some interest to him, of course; but if it is thick-trunked and beautiful, he is going to take it home with him even if nothing will ever appear on its branches but leaves.

Searching for material in a nursery is much the same. No matter how well stocked a local nursery is, the shopper is probably not going to find many of the particular species he has in mind. Looking for material by name, therefore, seems most often to be putting the cart before the horse. It does no harm to keep an eye out for a certain species, and sooner or later the grower may locate it. Meanwhile he would be wise to take the best of what he finds.

For these reasons it is hoped the following list will be used as the "cart" rather than the "horse." It has intentionally been kept as general as possible, with emphasis on the genera rather than the species. Unless otherwise indicated, these species are not difficult to find in large nurseries.

Pines have been handled in more detail, because one does not usually find a large local selection of them. They must often be ordered by mail from specialists. Also, unlike most conifers, the ease with which they may be grown and the needle length vary widely with the species.

Only species that have been grown by the writer are described here, so it is by no means a complete list of all promising bonsai material. Careful records have been kept of the good and bad features of each plant. It is from these records and from correspondence with a veteran Japanese grower that the following information was gathered.

Abelia An attractive, small-leaved shrub grown as bonsai principally for its pink or white tubular flowers, which appear in midsummer. Easy to grow. Deciduous. Some species not hardy.

AKEBIA, Five-leaf *(Akebia quinata)* Not a popular bonsai subject but grown by some Japanese experts for its interesting and unusual purple flowers and berries. Of twining habit, new shoots should be cut back to encourage bushiness. Akebias have large root systems but will stand severe root pruning in early spring. Deciduous. Hardy.

ALMOND, Flowering *(Prunus glandulosa)* The mass of small, pink flowers in early spring make the flowering almond well worth growing as a bonsai. Since trunk develops slowly, plant should be kept in open ground until of desired size. Deciduous. Hardy.

ARBORVITAE *(Thuja)* Because of their loose, spreading habits, most species do not make attractive bonsai. A few dwarf, dense varieties such as Little Gem *(T. occidentalis)* are exceptions and can be trained successfully. Conifer. Hardy.

Azalea   Small-flowered species are among the most popular of bonsai subjects. Easy to grow and beautiful in bloom. Best to start with as large a trunk as possible, since it will grow very slowly. Azaleas need an acid growing medium of pure peat moss or a mixture of peat, sand, and loam. Either seems to serve equally well. Repotting and branch trimming should be done immediately after spring blooming period. If shape will be improved by cutting some branches so short that no leaves are left on them, this may be done. New leaves will soon appear on the bare stems where no buds were apparent. Needs shade or part shade. Most species deciduous and hardy, but should be given some protection.

BAMBOO *(Bambusa)*   A pot of bamboo on the bonsai shelf adds charm and atmosphere to the whole collection. Easy to grow with but two basic requirements: plenty of water and protection from cold. Dwarf species are more desirable for pot culture. Eventually, the length of time depending on species and pot size, a bamboo root clump will become so large and solid it cannot be cut back enough to fit the same pot. A saw or sharp knife may then be used to divide it into two plants, or the whole clump may be moved, as it is, to a larger pot.

BARBERRY *(Berberis)*   The twisted shapes and bright autumn leaves of most species make good bonsai. They flower in spring and have berries in fall. Dwarf species such as the Japanese dwarf, *(B. microphylla koreana)* are especially suitable. Easy to grow. Both evergreen and deciduous species. Most deciduous species hardy.

BEECH *(Fagus)*   Leaves of most species are too large for successful dwarfing, but some varieties of European beech *(F. sylvatica)* are quite small and make excellent bonsai. Purple beech, cutleaf beech, and weeping beech are especially attractive. Deciduous. Hardy.

BIRCH, White *(Betula papyrifera)*   A beautiful grove of white birch trees in a shallow container is the first thing that comes to the minds of many beginners when selecting plants for dwarfing. Such a grove is easy to picture, but unfortunately not easy to grow. Short-lived in their natural state, birches have a much shorter life in a pot. Native to cold regions, perhaps some grower in a favorable area will be the first to produce a mature, dwarfed specimen of this attractive tree. Deciduous. Hardy.

BITTERSWEET *(Solanum dulcamara)*   A climbing plant that makes an interesting bonsai if kept trimmed back to encourage short, thick growth. Grown primarily for its bright orange berries. Deciduous. Hardy.

Box *(Buxus)*   A good subject for the beginner. Easy to grow and has naturally small leaves, especially the Korean variety *(B. microphylla koreana)*. Box is little respected by advanced growers, however, because no matter how expertly it is trained, it seldom has the *gei* of really fine bonsai. Since it is one of the few plants that has been grown indoors successfully, those who have no other facilities may want to try it on a window sill. Does best in part shade. Evergreen. Most species not reliably hardy.

CAROB or St. John's-Bread *(Ceratonia siliqua)*   There is only one species of this tree, said to date back to Biblical times. Makes an excellent dwarfed tree, with its rather small, round, leathery leaves. The hard brown pods, from which seeds may be obtained, are sold at many health-food stores as a chocolate substitute. Grows to a good-sized tree from seed in a few years. Does well in part shade but is not harmed by full sun and high temperatures. Evergreen. Not hardy.

CEDAR *(Cedrus)*   Of the three principal species, the Atlas cedar *(C. atlantica)* is the most popular for bonsai since it has dense clumps of small needles and is available in most nurseries. The cedar of Lebanon *(C. libana)* has somewhat longer needles, less dense growth habits, and is not widely sold. The Deodor cedar *(C. Deodara)* has the longest needles of the three species. Interesting varieties of cedar are available with weeping, contorted, or prostrate branches. Very easy to grow. New tips should be pinched back constantly. Conifer. Not reliably hardy in the North.

CHERRY, Flowering *(Prunus)* Many suitable species to choose from. All are spectacular in early spring, with their masses of small, pale pink flowers. Both weeping and erect varieties are available in many nurseries. Flowering cherries need a period of complete dormancy to bloom well, and are therefore not recommended for areas where winters are mild. Deciduous. Hardy.

Chrysanthemum Much has been written about producing bonsai from chrysanthemum plants in a single season. It seems to the writer that the results are not bonsai, but potted, blooming plants trained in the style of bonsai. The process of dwarfing is a slow one and cannot be completed in a single season.

CITRUS TREES Most citrus trees do not make the best bonsai. Leaves and fruit are usually too large, and growth habits suggest a potted plant rather than a dwarfed tree. Some species such as the Otaheite orange do bear small fruit and are occasionally grown as bonsai for this feature. Evergreen. Not hardy.

CORK TREE *(Phellodendron)* Often seen in nurseries, the cork tree is worth dwarfing only if a particularly good specimen is found. Otherwise, shade trees with smaller leaves give better results. Has an interesting, smooth trunk. Easy to grow. Deciduous. Hardy.

Corokia Cotoneaster The name is confusing, for this tree belongs to the *Corokia*, not the *Cotoneaster*, family. Although little known in most parts of the country, it is included because it makes such an excellent bonsai with its tiny leaves, gray-green above and white beneath, and many fine interlacing branchlets. Easy to grow. Evergreen. Not hardy.

Cotoneaster Many species of cotoneaster make excellent bonsai, as evidence by the fine old specimens of it in Japanese collections. All have small white or pink flowers in spring and clusters of red or black berries in fall. Probably the most often grown is the rock cotoneaster (*C. horizontalis*), a low, spreading plant with very small, semievergreen leaves and brilliant red fruit. Though not difficult to grow, cotoneasters can be tricky when conditions are not just right. They need plenty of water, but drainage in the pot must be excellent. Most species deciduous and hardy.

This *cotoneaster salicifolia* was more than six feet in diameter and about twenty years old when purchased from a nursery.

Roots were given plenty of room in which to recover from shock of transplanting.

Eight months later the tree has leafed out and crucial period is over.

Another year and tree is safely moved to its final container.

CRAB, Flowering (*Malus*) There are many species of crab to choose from, all small-flowered and attractive. Like most flowering fruit trees, the crab is grown primarily for its spring bloom, the buds of which form the previous fall. Pruning should therefore be done only in spring, immediately after the blooming period. Deciduous. Hardy.

CRAPE MYRTLE (*Lagerstroemia indica*) A popular bonsai subject because of its showy flowers that appear from middle to late summer, when few other bonsai are in bloom. Roots grow quickly, and when too crowded the plant will not bloom; so repotting must be done often, at least every spring and sometimes again in early fall. Food should be given more generously than with most other bonsai. To avoid cutting off next season's flower buds, plants should be pruned only after the blooming period. Crape myrtles, like lilacs, often grow from the ground with many thin stems, but one with a single thick trunk should be selected for dwarfing. Although this species will sometimes survive moderately cold winters in open ground, it should be considered not hardy when grown as a bonsai. Deciduous.

Cryptomeria One of the standard trees for bonsai. There is only one species, *japonica*, but eight or nine varieties are recognized, some with drooping branches, dwarf forms, etc. The natural shape is upright and pyramidal, and most dwarfed cryptomerias are trained in this way. Growth periods are prolonged, and new tips should be pinched back as they appear. Conifer. Not reliably hardy.

CYPRESS (*Cupressus*) and FALSE CYPRESS (*Chamaecyparis*) Most cypresses are easy to grow and make good bonsai. Arizona cypress (*C. arizonica*) and Monterey cypress (*C. macrocarpa*) are particularly good, with trunks that form naturally interesting shapes while still young. False cypresses, which prefer a slightly acid soil, offer a wide range of attractive and unusual trees. Two of the most popular are dwarf Hinoki cypress (*C. obtusa nana*), a very dense, compact tree that needs little shaping, and blue Hinoki cypress (*C. obtusa cyano viridis*), which has thick, feathery foliage ranging in different trees from blue-green to an almost unbelievable pale blue. The green thread-branch cypress (*C. pisifera filifera*) makes an unusual bonsai with long threadlike branches that should not be shortened, but trained to hang in a weeping style. Conifers. Although many species are listed as hardy, it is best to treat them as of doubtful hardiness when grown in pots.

Graceful drooping branches of green thread-branch cypress make this easy-to-grow tree a good species for bonsai. Right, the same tree, four years earlier.

CYPRESS, Bald *(Taxodium distichum)*   One of the few deciduous conifers, the bald cypress makes an interesting bonsai with its light, feathery foliage and cinnamon-colored bark. The long branches should be trimmed back to encourage dense growth and a neat form. Needs a great deal of water in spring and early summer. Setting the pot in a tray of water during this period is good practice. Not reliably hardy in the North.

DOGWOOD, Flowering *(Cornus florida)* Dogwoods are not often grown as bonsai because of their rather large, widely spaced leaves. Their beautiful spring flowers, appearing before the leaves, have persuaded some growers to dwarf them. Deciduous. Hardy.

Elaeagnus pungens There is no common name for this excellent bonsai subject. Though not widely sold, it can be found in some nurseries. The small, wavy-edged leaves are silvery beneath and glossy above, with green centers and creamy white edges. Most attractive and unusual. Easy to grow. Evergreen. Not hardy.

ELM *(Ulmus)* Small-leaved species are among the best of all trees for bonsai. Very easy to grow and train. Two of the most popular species are the Japanese elm *(U. japonica)* and Chinese elm *(U. parvifolia)*, both of which are listed as the widely grown Nire elm of Japanese bonsai. The Siberian or dwarf elm *(U. pumila)* and the winged or Wahoo elm *(U. alata)* with its interesting, corky branchlets are other good species. The most important feature of a well-trained, dwarfed elm is its dense, twiggy crown, which is admired when bare in winter as much as when in full leaf. Tips should be pinched back constantly to encourage branching. Deciduous. All species named here are very hardy, with the exception of the winged elm.

EUCALYPTUS, Silver Dollar *(Eucalyptus cinerea)* An attractive tree with small, round, silvery-gray leaves on flexible branches. Since trunk size increases slowly, young trees should be grown in the ground in mild climates until large enough for potting. Evergreen. Of easy culture, but not hardy.

Eurya Another little-known tree with excellent possibilities. Small, shining, leathery leaves and small white flowers. Easily grown. Does best in part shade. Evergreen. Not hardy.

FIG *(Ficus)* One species, the weeping fig *(F. benjamina)* with its small, shining leaves and gracefully drooping branches, is especially suitable for bonsai. An evergreen, it grows quickly and is of easy cultivation. The common fig *(F. carica)*, a deciduous tree, is too coarse and large-leaved for successful dwarfing; although it bears fruit readily in pots and may interest the grower for this reason. None hardy.

From little more than a seedling, this weeping fig grew into a good-size tree in just twenty-four months.

Starting summer growth in June.

Three months later, September.

The following August. First picture (above left) was taken ten months later, again in June.

FIR *(Abies)*   Many fir trees make good bonsai. The white fir *(A. concolor)* is popular for dwarfing. Firs are similar in appearance to spruces, although they need more water and should be grown in part shade. Tips of new growth should be pinched back as it appears. Conifer. Hardy.

FIR, Douglas *(Pseudotsuga taxifolia)*   Another good bonsai subject with the same growing requirements as the *Abies*, but differing from them in botanical classification. Conifer. Hardy.

FIRETHORN *(Pyracantha)*   An excellent, easy-to-grow shrub with clusters of white flowers in early spring and bright orange or red berries in fall. If there is a heavy crop of berries the plant may not fruit well, if at all, the following year. Cutting berries off when they are just past their prime will help to encourage annual bloom and fruit. Evergreen. Few species hardy.

Forsythia   Well worth growing as bonsai for the profusion of yellow flowers in spring. Many species to choose from, some with dwarf, some with weeping habits. Deciduous. Hardy.

Ginkgo   SEE MAIDENHAIR TREE

GUAVA, Strawberry *(Psidium cattleianum)*   The small fruit, best known for the jelly made from it, and smooth, glossy leaves of this tree make it well worth growing as a bonsai. Of easy cultivation but rather slow growing. Evergreen. Not hardy.

HACKBERRY *(Celtis)*   The small-leaved species make excellent bonsai. In their natural state they reseed readily, so that interesting specimens are often found in an area where mature trees are growing. They have long tap roots but withstand severe root pruning in early spring. Not particular as to growing conditions. Deciduous. Hardy.

HAWTHORN *(Crataegus)*   A slow-growing, small tree with appropriately small leaves and fruit. Good for bonsai if a fairly large specimen can be found to start with. There are numerous species to choose from, all deciduous. Most are hardy.

HAZELNUT, Contorted *(Corylus avellana contorta)*   Said to be the tree from which Harry Lauder, the Scottish singer, obtained the snakelike, twisted cane that was his trademark. This is believable, for the branches twist and turn in a most interesting way. It is often found in nurseries because of this eye-catching characteristic. Unfortunately the leaves are rather coarse and large, a handicap some growers ignore because of its unusual shape. Deciduous. Hardy.

HEMLOCK *(Tsuga)*   Although a most tempting tree because of its delicate, fine foliage, in the writer's experience the hemlock is difficult to grow in a small container. This may explain why there are no pictures of famous old bonsai of this genus to be found. Conifer. Some species completely hardy, others less so in very cold areas.

HOLLY *(Ilex)*   There is such a variety of hollies to choose from, all with bright berries, that every grower will want at least one before he is very far along. Leaves of the small-leaved species usually do not have the prominent, spiny teeth associated with the holly of Christmas decorations. The Yaupon *(I. vomitoria)* is particularly suitable, with its miniature leaves and numerous branchlets. Hollies seem to prefer an acid soil, so the addition of peat moss to the potting mixture is recommended. Both deciduous and evergreen, hardy and nonhardy species.

HOLLY, False *(Osmanthus ilicifolius)*   For those who prefer the traditional spiny holly leaf, the false holly is a more desirable tree for dwarfing than the American holly since its dark-green, shiny leaves are comparatively small. Evergreen. Of easy culture, but not hardy.

HORNBEAM *(Carpinus)*   Like most deciduous shade trees, the hornbeam is a good tree for bonsai if a small-leaved species, such as *C. laxiflora*, is selected. A few beautiful dwarfed hornbeams are among the prized old bonsai of Japan. Of easy culture. Hardy.

IVY *(Parthenocissus* and *Hedera)*   Old, thick-stemmed ivy makes a very attractive bonsai if it fulfills the usual requirements of having small leaves. Ivy stems thicken slowly in pots, however, so an old, twisted specimen should be found to start with. The trailing ends should be pinched back constantly to encourage bushy growth. If the grower has been able to grow ivy successfully in the house, he can train an ivy bonsai just as easily in the same location. Most species require shade or part shade and plenty of moisture. Some are deciduous, some evergreen. There are both hardy and nonhardy species.

Jacaranda   This tree with its delicate, lacy leaves makes a very attractive bonsai. However, since it must be of a certain size to bloom, it is almost impossible to produce both a dwarfed tree and flowers. Grows easily from seed, and the trunk becomes quite large in just a few years. Has a tendency to become too tall if the top is not cut back constantly. Deciduous. Not hardy.

JUNIPER (*Juniperus*)   Popular with beginners and advanced growers alike, since it is probably the easiest of all conifers to grow yet requires skill to train into a successful bonsai. If the tips are not pinched back constantly, most species will become loose

Juniperus procumbens, a very hardy species with needle-like foilage, is an excellant subject for bonsai.

and spreading. The growth habits of some, such as the *Hetzi* and *Pfitzer*, are such that they have little *gei*, even when carefully trained. Species most often used for bonsai are the Sargent juniper (*J. chinensis sargentii*) and the needle juniper (*J. rigida*). In addition, there are many varieties constantly being developed and sold that are not listed in standard botanical dictionaries but make excellent bonsai. Whatever the species, desirable characteristics are tight, dense growth and rather stiff needles. All junipers have small root systems that renew themselves readily when pruned. Plenty of sunlight will discourage the tendency of these trees to become "leggy." If this does occur, unlike most conifers they may be trimmed back as desired and new growth will soon appear. Most are hardy.

Keaki Elm   See *Zelkova*

Larch (*Larix*)   Another deciduous member of the pine family. Although not used for bonsai as often as some other conifers, their light-green, soft, needle-like foliage is very attractive if kept trimmed back to encourage dense growth. Although very similar in appearance, the Japanese larch (*L. leptolepis*) seems to withstand root pruning more readily than does the Tamarack or American larch (*L. laricina*). Hardy.

Linden (*Tilia*)   The leaves of most linden trees are too large for successful dwarfing. Two species, however, the littleleaf or small-leaved linden (*T. cordata*) and the Japanese linden (*T. japonica*), have small enough leaves for bonsai. Neat, close growth habits make these trees well worth trying. Easy to grow, but need plenty of moisture. Deciduous. Hardy.

Locust (*Robinia*)   The two species most commonly found in nurseries are the black locust (*R. pseudoacacia*) and the rose acacia or pink sweet pea tree (*R. hispida*). Although very similar in appearance when potted, the black locust in its natural state grows to a height of eighty feet, while the rose acacia is more shrublike. Because of their small, oval leaflets they make interesting bonsai if new shoots are pinched back constantly to en-

courage the formation of twigs. Easy to grow. Deciduous.
Hardy.

LOCUST, Honey *(Gleditsia triacanthos)*   Similar in growth habits
to the *Robinia*, the leaflets of the honey locust are narrower
and more closely spaced. Like many common shade trees,
young locusts can usually be found in a neighborhood where
mature specimens are growing. Little is lost if a few of these
are moved to a corner of the garden and allowed to develop for
a few years. Some may turn out to be excellent dwarfed trees.
Deciduous. Hardy.

Magnolia   Because of its large leaves, the magnolia is not a popular
bonsai subject. However, a well-shaped specimen, its fragrant
flowers appearing before the leaves, can be very beautiful when
dwarfed. *M. stellata*, a deciduous tree, has smaller-than-average
leaves and is probably the species most used for bonsai. Magno-
lias do not transplant easily and should only be moved before
the leaves appear in spring. Both deciduous and evergreen species, the evergreens not hardy.

MAIDENHAIR TREE *(Ginkgo biloba)*   One of the standard, popular
trees for bonsai. Its unusual, fan-shaped leaves, which turn
bright yellow in fall, are a little larger than ideal for dwarfing.
Their neat, close growth and other desirable features more than
make up for this one shortcoming. Very easy to grow, and do
well in pots from a few inches in diameter to very large sizes.
Need plenty of sun and water. Deciduous. Hardy.

MAPLE *(Acer)*   All small-leaved maples make excellent bonsai.
They are of easy culture, may be severely root-pruned in early
spring, and promising specimens can be found readily in every
nursery or growing naturally. Little is lacking to make them
ideal subjects. A few of the good species for bonsai are: Amur
scarlet maple *(A. Ginnala)*, fullmoon maple *(A. japonicum)*,
trident maple *(A. Buergerianum)*, any varieties of the fernleaf
maple *(A. japonicum acontifolium)*, and the red-leaved varieties of the Japanese maple *(A. palmatum)*. Deciduous. All spe-

cies given here are hardy, although small branches of the fern-leaf maple may be injured by very low temperatures.

MIMOSA *or* SILK-TREE *(Albizzia Julibrissin)*   Any grower who has a large mimosa tree in his garden will not be able to resist trying to dwarf one or two of the many small ones that spring up everywhere from seed. Like the jacaranda it is almost impossible to make them bloom in pots, but their fairly rapid growth, easy culture, and small leaves make them interesting, if not ideal, subjects. Deciduous. Not hardy in extremely cold areas.

MULBERRY *(Morus)*   Although mulberry leaves and trunks dwarf readily, the trees have long tap roots and comparatively few fibrous roots. This is a situation not ideal for the limited space in a small container. The trees live, but leaves become sparse and growth is slow. Deciduous. Hardy.

NANDINA *(Nandina domestica)*   Called "Heavenly bamboo" in China. An attractive shrub, evergreen in warm climates, with rather thinly spaced leaves that turn brilliant red in autumn. Sometimes grown as a bonsai for this fall color. Needs plenty of water. Not hardy.

OAK *(Quercus)*   In general, leaves of most species of oak are too large for dwarfing, although a few fine old bonsai with relatively large leaves do exist. The cork oak *(Q. Suber)*, which yields commercial cork, has appropriately small leaves and makes an excellent bonsai, but is not easy to find. The live oak *(Q. virginiana)*, with somewhat larger leaves, also dwarfs very well. Oaks have few fibrous roots, so care should be taken in transplanting. Deciduous and evergreen. Most deciduous species are hardy, the evergreen not.

ORCHID TREE *(Bauhinia variegata)*   Often included in catalogues advertising bonsai stock, this tree does not seem to be first-rate bonsai material. It has interesting, round, lobed leaves and orchidlike flowers, but trunk grows very slowly and leaves are thinly spaced. Deciduous. Not hardy.

PAGODA TREE, JAPANESE *or* CHINESE SCHOLAR TREE *(Sophora*

japonica)   Attractive, small, pinnate leaves, relatively fast-growing trunk. Of easy culture. A good subject. Deciduous. Hardy.

PEACH *(Prunus Persica)*   Two five-year-old peach trees grown from seed now have good thick trunks, heavy branches with few twigs, rather long thin leaves, but little *gei*. Smaller leaved, flowering fruit trees are more desirable as bonsai. Deciduous. Of doubtful hardiness.

PEPPER-TREE *(Schinus Molle)*   Grows easily from seed and develops a good trunk in a few years. Toothed leaves are thin and graceful, with a peppery fragrance when crushed. A good subject. Evergreen. Not hardy.

PERSIMMON *(Diospyros)*   There are only two species of persimmon with edible fruit: the common persimmon *(D. virginiana)* and the Kaki, or Japanese persimmon *(D. chinensis)*. Both have leaves and fruit that are somewhat large for successful bonsai. Deciduous. Only the common persimmon is hardy.

Pieris japonica   A popular bonsai subject. Slender, evergreen leaves and panicles of white, urn-shaped flowers that open in spring from buds formed the previous summer. Blooms well even when dwarfed. Should be grown in part shade and given plenty of water. Hardy.

Pieris japonica, showing buds that form one year, open the next. Flowers resemble lilies of the valley.

PINE *(Pinus)* A perfectly trained, dwarfed pine tree is probably the highest from of the art of bonsai. One has only to compare the price of a beautiful dwarfed pine with that of any other tree to realize how much pines are valued. Fine specimens sold commercially may range in price from a few hundred to four or five thousand dollars each. Though not difficult, they are not the easiest trees to grow; but they have a natural *gei* that simplifies the work of shaping them. In addition they normally have only one growth period a year, so there is no need for constant summer control of their branches. Except in very young trees, new growth is slow and small. It is usually confined to the tips of existing branches, so that the careful training of past years is not lost in a maze of new shoots.

Whether the grower loves all pines, long- and short-needled, or prefers only those with small needles that, when dwarfed, will be in proportion to the trunk, is a matter of personal taste. However, to shorten the long needles of a pine by cutting them, a method sometimes recommended, is very poor bonsai practice.

Once a pine has become well established in its container, it is not difficult to maintain in good health indefinitely. Young pines, however, and especially seedlings, are more susceptible to unfavorable growing conditions. All pines, young and old alike, show injury so slowly that even when it proves fatal, they seem not to die but, like old soldiers, to "just fade away." Unfortunately, once this fading is noticed, it is often too late to save the tree.

Care should be taken not to overfeed a dwarfed pine, for it may then put out a scattering of needles that have reverted to their normal length. Such needles can be plucked out, one by one, but it is best to avoid the occurrence altogether.

Of the forty-odd species of pine the writer has grown as bonsai, the following are worthy of comment either pro or con:

BISHOP *(P. muricata)* Long-needled, dense, fast-growing. A fair subject. Of doubtful hardiness.

BRUTIA *(P. halepensis brutia)* Short-needled, dense. Good subject. Not hardy.

CANARY ISLAND *(P. canariensis)* Long-needled. Unusual, light-green color. Difficult to grow. Of doubtful hardiness.

DIGGER *(P. Sabiniana)* Long, bluish needles. Dwarfs well. Of doubtful hardiness.

HICKORY, Bristlecone or Aristata *(P. aristata)* Excellent short-needled subject but very difficult to establish. Slow-growing. Of doubtful hardiness.

HIMALAYAN WHITE *(P. nepalensis)* Long, soft, drooping needles with flexible, easily shaped trunks and branches. Easy to grow and very hardy.

ITALIAN STONE *(P. Pinea)* Medium needles. Like all stone pines, has attractive, irregularly shaped trunk and branches. Good subject. Easy to grow. Of doubtful hardiness.

JACK *(P. Banksiana)* Short, dense, slightly curled needles. Fairly slow-growing. Good subject. Hardy.

JAPANESE BLACK *(P. Thunbergii)* A popular tree for bonsai. Medium needles. Easy to grow. Hardy.

JAPANESE RED *(P. resinosa)* Medium needles. Much used for bonsai, but difficult to establish. Sensitive to polluted air. Hardy.

JAPANESE WHITE or FIVE-NEEDLE *(P. parviflora)* One of the best for bonsai but, except for seedlings, difficult to find. More expensive than most pines. Seedlings delicate; older trees, or those grafted on black-pine stock, easy to grow. Hardy.

JEFFREY *(P. Jeffreyi)* Long, coarse needles. Not recommended. Hardy.

KNOBCONE *(P. attenuata)* Long needles, fine and drooping. Easy to grow. Hardy.

KOREAN *(P. koraiensis)* Medium needles, interestingly curved. Good subject but rather slow-growing. Of doubtful hardiness.

LIMBER *(P. flexilis)*   Short-needled. Slow, rather dense growth. Good subject. Hardy.

LOBLOLLY *(P. Taeda)*   Growing a Loblolly pine for its name alone is a temptation. Long, thin, curved needles, not very dense. Easy to grow. Of doubtful hardiness.

LONGLEAF *(P. palustris)*   Graceful, drooping needles to eighteen inches long. A beautiful and unusual eyecatcher for pot culture, if not for bonsai. Not hardy.

MEXICAN PINON *(P. cembroides)*   Short-needled. Slow-growing. Good subject but not of easy culture. Not hardy.

MONTEREY *(P. radiata)*   Medium-long needles, but dense and graceful. Easy to grow. Of doubtful hardiness.

MUGHO or SWISS MOUNTAIN *(P. Mugo)*   Short-needled, moderately slow-growing. Of easy culture; a good subject. Can be found in most nurseries. Hardy.

NORFOLK ISLAND *(Araucaria excelsa)*   Not classified botanically as a pine. Allowed to grow naturally, this short-needled tree is symmetrical and columnar, with branches radiating like wheel spokes at regular intervals up the trunk. Experiments have shown, however, that with constant pinching back the tree becomes dense and irregular and promises to be an interesting and attractive bonsai. Not hardy.

SCOTS *(P. sylvestris)*   Fairly short needles, light green and twisted. A good subject, particularly the dwarf variety *(P. sylvestris pumila)*. Very hardy.

SCRUB *(P. virginiana)*   Stiff, fairly long needles. Not recommended. Hardy.

SHORE *(P. contorta)*   Short, twisted needles. A good subject but not easy to grow. Not reliably hardy.

SLASH *(P. caribaea)*   Long-needled, fast-growing. Not recommended. Hardy.

SUGAR *(P. Lambertiana) Medium needles, rather dense* growth. A fair subject but many others are better. Of doubtful hardiness.

SWISS STONE (*P. Cembra*)   Medium needles. All stone pines
make interesting subjects because of their flexibility and irregular shapes. Hardy, but grows more slowly in cold areas.

Left, still in the process of being dwarfed, this Swiss stone pine is shown
as it was developed over a period of three years. Center, freshly dug from
the ground, it recovers in a large pot. Right, eighteen months later,
pruning and transplanting are completed.

TABLE MOUNTAIN (*P. pungens*)   Short, stiff, twisted needles.
Good subject. Semihardy.

WESTERN YELLOW (*P. ponderosa*)   Long, thick, coarse needles. Not recommended. Hardy.

WHITE (*P. Strobus*)   Long, fine, graceful needles but not dense
enough to make good bonsai. Dwarf forms are listed, however, that may be more desirable. Hardy.

PLUM, Natal *(Carissa grandiflora)*   An attractive tree with small, glossy, leathery leaves; milky juice; and very fragrant, star-shaped flowers. Trunk develops slowly. Easy to grow and a good subject. Best in part shade. Evergreen. Not hardy.

Podocarpus   Though sometimes grown as a bonsai, this conifer suggests to the writer a potted house plant rather than a dwarfed tree. Only the small-leaved species should be selected for dwarfing. Not hardy.

POMEGRANATE *(Punica Granatum)*   One of the very good trees for bonsai in warm areas or for growing under glass. Easy to grow and withstands severe root pruning. The brilliant, orange-red flowers and yellow or red fruit develop on the ends of new shoots, so care should be taken when pruning. (See the notes on pruning pomegranates.) Growers not acquainted with the flower buds often mistake them for fruit since they are round, hard balls that turn from green to orange before opening. Deciduous. Not hardy.

Pyracantha   SEE FIRETHORN

QUINCE, Flowering *(Chaenomeles,* often listed as *Cydonia)*   Of

The flowering quince grows in a naturally interesting shape, blooms freely, and is very easy to care for; three qualities that make it an excellent subject for beginners.

very easy culture and therefore an excellent subject for the beginner. Its spiny, irregular branches grow in interesting shapes. In early spring, before leaves appear, showy flowers stand out brilliantly against the bare branches. Even very young plants usually bloom, in colors ranging from white to bright orange or red. In fact, producing good bonsai from flowering quince requires so little skill that it is usually passed up by advanced growers in favor of more challenging material. Deciduous or semievergreen. Hardy.

REDBUD or JUDAS TREE *(Cercis)*   Because of leaf size, the redbud is a borderline tree for bonsai; but if a good specimen is found, it should be tried. Grows well in pots. Leaves turn bright yellow in fall. Deciduous. Hardy except in extremely cold areas.

REDWOOD, Dawn *(Metasequoia)*   The shape and feathery foliage of this tree resemble those of the bald cypress, to which it is related. Culture of both trees is much the same, although the dawn redwood needs only normal watering and its roots cannot stand such severe pruning. Deciduous. Semihardy.

REDWOOD *(Sequoia sempervirens)*   The redwood and the giant Sequoia are very difficult to keep alive in pots for more than a few years, which may explain why there are no well-known bonsai of this genus. Evergreen. Not hardy.

Rhododendron   Belonging to the same family as the azaleas, rhododendrons have the same requirements of an acid potting soil and protection from direct sunlight. Many species are too large-leaved for successful bonsai, but there are a number of smaller-leaved species, such as R. *Augustinii,* that are very desirable. While most azaleas are deciduous, rhododendrons are usually evergreen. Both hardy and nonhardy species.

SEQUOIA, Giant *(Sequoiadendron giganteum)*   SEE REDWOOD

SILVER-BELL or SNOWDROP TREE *(Halesia)*   Another easy-to-grow tree with attractive, drooping clusters of white, bell-shaped flowers in early spring. Flowers develop on previous year's branches. Stands transplanting and root pruning well. Again, the drawback of rather large leaves, overlooked by some growers because of the bloom. Deciduous. Both hardy and nonhardy species.

SMOKE-TREE *(Cotinus Coggygria)*   Sometimes listed as *Rhus Cotinus*. A good subject because of its small, unusual leaves, which are nearly round, white-ribbed, and white- or red-edged. The variety C. *purpureus* has purple leaves, and C. *pendulas* has drooping branches. In midsummer loose, hairlike panicles appear on mature trees. These panicles resemble puffs of smoke, giving the tree its name. Deciduous. Hardy.

SPINDLE TREE *(Euonymous)*   There are many species of the spindle tree to choose from, some that grow naturally as trees, some as shrubs, some hardy, some not. A few very old bonsai of this genus exist. None are difficult to grow, with average soil and water needs. The branches of E. *alatus* develop interesting, corky wings. The well-known E. *patens* is of particularly easy culture, with roots that survive in pots as small as an inch in diameter. Most species evergreen and hardy.

SPRUCE *(Picea)*   A popular subject, with the small needles and dense growth desirably for bonsai. Spruces are similar to firs in appearance, but unlike firs they need a great deal of sun and less water. Species most often used for dwarfing are: white spruce *(P. glauca)*, with slightly drooping branches; Yedo spruce *(P. jezoensis)*, which is not as easy to find but probably the most sought-after species for bonsai; Alberta spruce *(P. glauca albertiana)* and its dwarf variety *(P. glauca nana)*: Black Hills spruce *(P. glauca densata)*; Colorado blue spruce *(P. pungens)*; and the Norway spruce *(P. Abies)*. The needles of the Koster blue spruce, a variety of P. *pungens*, are larger and stiffer than those of most other species but have the best color, a very light gray-blue. Conifers. Hardy.

SWEETGUM *(Liquidambar Styraciflua)*   An attractive tree, sometimes mistaken for a maple because of the leaf shape, but with a root system more like that of the oak. When lifting from the ground for the first time, both top and roots should be cut back to maintain balance, since sweetgums do not transplant as easily as most deciduous trees. If grown in the garden for a few years, the tree should be dug and replanted each spring to keep fibrous roots as close to the base of the trunk as possible. Should be repotted only in early spring. Deciduous. Not reliably hardy in cold areas.

TALLOW-TREE, Chinese *(Sapium sebiferum)*   A four-year-old tree of this species grown from seed has turned out to be a pleasant surprise. The curious, bottle-shaped trunk is more than one-and-a-half inches across at its base. The glossy, leathery leaves are prominently white-veined, touched with red at the edges and beneath. It withstands full, hot sun and needs a minimum amount of water. With its stiff, erect habits it may not have *gei* as a bonsai in future years, but it is a most interesting tree. Evergreen. Not hardy.

WILLOW *(Salix)*   Although the weeping willow *(S. babylonica)* is a popular bonsai subject, its needs, simple but important, are often misunderstood by beginners, who may then have little success with it. The long, pendant branches are important. They should never be shortened, but trained to hang in curving arches by weights or wires. If growth becomes too thick, thinning may be done by removing whole branches. All willows need almost unlimited amounts of water, especially during growing periods. Pots should be set in trays of water from spring until growth slows down in midsummer. Trees may live but upper branches will die if only a normal amount of water is given at this time. Willow roots grow quickly, so trees should not be planted in very small pots. They should be repotted every spring and checked for another possible repotting in early fall. The increasingly popular corkscrew willow *(S. Matsudana tortuosa)* has the same needs. Its growth habit is more erect, and the long, twisted branches may be kept trimmed back to encourage bushiness if desired. Even when properly trained, it does not seem to have as much *gei* as the weeping willow. Deciduous. Most species hardy.

Wistaria   Another popular bonsai subject, grown principally for its spectacular flowers in early spring. After the blooming period the plant is usually set aside, for unless the trunk is very unusual, it is not particularly attractive during the summer months. Some species, usually grafted, bloom before leaves appear in spring. These must be of a certain size, not age, before they will flower. The racemes of flowers that appear on other species after the leaves have opened are usually shorter, but such plants will often bloom while still quite young and small. To insure full bloom the following spring, new shoots should be pinched back constantly all summer to one or two buds, except where a long branch is needed to improve shape. Plenty of sun and water should be given. Repotting is done immediately after the blooming period. Deciduous. Most species hardy.

Yew *(Taxus)*   Because of their bushy, upright habits, most species of yew do not make good bonsai. Some varieties of the Japanese yew *(T. cuspidata)* and the English yew *(T. baccata)* are exceptions. Trees with thick, curving trunks and interesting main branches should be selected. Pruning should be heavy to reveal their lines. New growth should be pinched back to a few needles, as this encourages thick, neat clumps. Yews have many fibrous roots and are easy to grow. They do best in part shade. Conifers. Hardy.

Zelkova, Japanese Gray-Bark Elm, Keaki, Keyaki *(Zelkova serrata)*   One of the trees most used for Japanese bonsai, the zelkova is very similar in appearance to the elm but differs from it in botanical classification. An easy-to-grow, deciduous tree, it is usually trained with an erect trunk and a dense crown, solid with twigs. Hardy.

INDEX